THE
GREEN CASE

THE
GREEN CASE

A sociology of environmental
issues, arguments and politics

Steven Yearley

Department of Social Studies
The Queen's University of Belfast

HarperCollins*Academic*
An Imprint of HarperCollins*Publishers*

Published by
HarperCollins*Academic*

77-85 Fulham Palace Road
Hammersmith
London W6 8JB
UK

First published in 1991

British Library Cataloguing in Publication Data
Yearley, Steven
The green case : a sociology of environmental issues,
arguments and politics.
1. Environment. Sociopolitical aspects
I. Title
304.2
ISBN 0-04-445752-9

Library of Congress Cataloging in Publication Data
Yearley, Steven.
The green case : a sociology of environmental issues,
arguments, and politics / Steven Yearley.
p. cm.
Includes bibliographical references and index.
ISBN 0-04-445751-0 : $44.95.
ISBN 0-04-445752-9 (pbk.) : $16.95
1. Green movement. 2. Environmental policy. 3. Marketing—
Social aspects. 4. Economic development—Environmental aspects.
I. Title.
JA75.8.Y43 1991
322.4'4—dc20
90-45469
CIP

Typeset in 10 on 12 point Sabon
Printed in Great Britain by
Billing & Sons Ltd, London and Worcester

Contents

Acknowledgements

I would like to record my thanks to several people who helped me during the writing of this book. I received a great deal of patient assistance from staff in the library at Queen's University Belfast, notably the periodicals librarians, the inter-library loans staff and Nigel Butterwick. My initial research on scientific expertise and scientific authority in the green movement was supported by the Science Policy Support Group (SPSG) and the Economic and Social Research Council; I would like to thank the staff of SPSG and the other participants in the programme on the Public Understanding of Science for their support and friendship during that research. Many thanks are also due to the people in the environmental movement who explained things to me, welcomed me into their meetings and showed me round their nature reserves. Lastly, my thanks go to my colleague Steve Bruce who read much of this book in draft and who offered me a great deal of sound sociological advice.

INTRODUCTION

Studying the green case

By the end of the 1980s environmental awareness had become widespread, popular and fashionable throughout the Western world. In Eastern Europe the environmental cause had become closely identified with movements campaigning for a reduction in the power of the state. This confluence is perhaps best expressed in the name of the Bulgarian environmental protest group 'Ecoglasnost' (*Guardian* 2 November 1989, p. 7). It is now good to be 'green'. The environment is suddenly on everybody's agenda: it has been adopted by politicians, by manufacturers, by teachers, by advertising agencies and by publishers. This book sets out to explain why the 'green wave' has started rolling now and to examine the forces shaping the future of green politics and policies on an international scale.

Politicians seldom act without thought of electoral advantage so the scramble by parties of right and left to display their policies as environmentally friendly stands as testimony to the perceived public interest in the environment. In Britain, probably the most conspicuous reflection of this interest was the pair of speeches made in late September and early October 1988 by the Conservative Prime Minister, Margaret Thatcher. In these two addresses, one to the Royal Society (the UK's foremost scientific society), the other to the Conservative Party Conference, she sought to align Tory traditionalism with conservation. Labour politicians responded by emphasizing the link between their penchant for social interventionism and the kinds of regulation needed to protect the environment. Seemingly incontestable evidence of growing public enthusiasm was also supplied by the electoral performance of the UK's Green Party in the 1989 elections for the European Parliament, in which they captured an unexpectedly large share (14.5 per cent) of the vote.[1] Being seen as reasonably 'green' is an increasingly successful political strategy.

Sensitive to public opinion as they may be, politicians are not quite as responsive as people who have to court the public on a day-by-day basis, including the media and advertisers. Advertising agencies' attempts to win the 'green consumer' are a rich resource for the analyst of changing social attitudes, both because their work has to be arresting and attractive in its own right, and because advertisements often carry a heavy burden of implicit meanings or connotations. Humorous treatments of environmental issues quickly appeared: the British motor company Vauxhall (a subsidiary of General Motors, sought to cash in on two fashions of 1989 by describing its convertible model as 'lid free'. Soft tops were in vogue as were campaigns to promote the use of lead-free petrol; the slogan marries the fashions.

More elaborately, during 1989 the French-based company Peaudouce ran a series of advertisements for their nappies, promoting them because the dressings were not made from chlorine-bleached materials. The use of chlorine as a bleaching agent can lead to the formation of compounds in the product which may be injurious to the user's health; related toxic compounds can also be discharged into the environment from the effluent. Beneath a picture of a smiling toddler, happily swathed in such a nappy, was the caption, 'eau-zone friendly' (comparable wit was displayed by the manufacturers of 'Right Guard' deodorant who labelled their product as 'nose-zone friendly').

Although the pun is rather contrived, the advertisement is revealing in a number of ways. First, it works on the assumption that shoppers will know about the supposed dangers of the use of chlorine. This issue is not addressed in the text of the advertisement. Second, it seems to presume that danger to health, and possibly the wider question of toxic discharges from the manufacturing by-products, are of the greatest importance to people; thus, the price and effectiveness of the product are not mentioned in this advertisement. Finally, and most revealing, it is assumed that people will know about threats to the ozone layer and about the preceding campaign to persuade shoppers to buy only 'ozone-friendly' aerosols (sprays which are not propelled by CFCs, see Chapter 1) *and* that they will class this as a related issue. In other words it seems to be assumed that consumers regard environmental issues as linked and that their concerns about these problems are mutually reinforcing.

WHAT IS GREEN?

The rise of environmental awareness is clearly a social phenomenon of major proportions. As I have already said, one aim of this book is to clarify and explain how and why this awareness has developed. At the same time it is important not to take for granted the coherence of the green phenomenon. As the Peaudouce case illustrates, there appears to be a set of problem issues which have become associated in the public mind. Of course, both chlorine bleaching and the depletion of the ozone layer can readily be interpreted as central environmental problems. It is probably possible to identify a list of more-or-less agreed central environmental issues. And the sense that they are closely related is no doubt enhanced by some of the complexities thrown up by the natural world. Thus, concern about ozone has entered the public's conscience through the destruction of the ozone layer, high up in the atmosphere. But our technologies also cause ozone gas to be produced in the lower atmosphere. For example, it is formed by the electrical discharges in photocopiers and by the interaction of exhaust fumes with ultra-violet radiation from the sun (*Guardian* 29 January 1990, p. 17). Low-level ozone is a possible health risk; it also contributes to global warming. Relatively high concentrations of low-level ozone are found in the 'photochemical smogs' formed over large, traffic-filled cities (this pollution is also known by the name 'Los Angeles smog'). With the rise in concern over low-level ozone, environmentalists have the difficult job of persuading the public, newly informed of the value of this gas, that its accidental production at ground level is as undesirable as its unplanned depletion high in the atmosphere.

Such overlaps may cause confusion. But they also indicate how difficult it is to put a boundary round environmental questions, to determine what is a green issue and what is not. And this boundary problem is further exacerbated by commercial concerns which have discovered the consumer appeal of ecologically sound and 'natural' products. These businesses have accordingly tried to lever as many products as possible into the range of items seen as environmentally related. An astonishing range of products is now described as 'environment friendly', 'friendly to wildlife' or full of 'natural goodness'. In Britain we have long had the benefit of 'natural yoghurt'; in this case natural appears to be a flavour, since such yoghurts can still be called 'natural' even if they are well stocked with preservatives. In 1989, Tate and Lyle's white sugar bore the legend, 'granulated cane sugar' while underneath in facsimile handwriting was printed, 'from natural cane'. Conceivably, the sugar processing company was keen to dispel the notion that white sugar was a synthetic, purely industrial product. But the caption does appear to imply that there could be such a thing as *unnatural* cane.

The food industry has clearly found the notion of naturalness attractive; many consumers are after all increasingly concerned about the connection between diet and health. But these producers have been joined by the world of interior design (paints now come in natural shades) and by the cosmetics industry. Nearly all cosmetics offer to lend a natural beauty (on 'natural' beauty and femininity see Williamson 1978, pp. 123–37). In the new merchandising cosmology, products seem either to be natural or non-natural. The former are good, the latter are to be avoided. Of course, some products can be sold as non-natural – as 'made things' – and their artefactuality celebrated. In British commercials, Volkswagen has cleverly advertised its cars as being full of preservatives and thick with colourings. But in general, manufacturers are presenting more and more products as natural. Indeed, as will be seen in Chapter 3, products whose connection with issues such as global warming or ozone depletion is very remote or non-existent are presented as contributing to the green revolution.[2]

Even setting aside these over-imaginative extensions of the notion, it is hard to define which issues are green ones and which are not. Thus, it would be quite reasonable to accept that wildlife conservation groups (such as the Royal Society for the Protection of Birds (RSPB) or the Marine Conservation Society) and more general environmental protection organizations (like Greenpeace) are central to the movement. But the status of other groups is more contentious. Simply as an illustration, the Vegetarian Society has much in common with the green movement and there are influential environmental arguments for vegetarianism; but not all environmentalists are vegetarian, neither are all vegetarians environmentally active. Another well-known example is the Royal Society for the Prevention of Cruelty to Animals (RSPCA). It clearly has much in common with nature conservation organizations and works with them in opposing such practices as badger-baiting and in rescuing animals from environmental disasters. But its focus tends to be on individual animals rather than on species or habitats; its brief is not an environmental one. Then again there are groups with interests in aspects of the environment because of the amenities it offers: groups representing the interests of ramblers, climbers and even mountain-bikers. There are also those whose aim it is to preserve the beauty of the countryside rather than to safeguard wildlife *per se*.

Amongst the most difficult cases to classify are those presented by various sporting associations. The case of fox hunting is very well known: its proponents argue that the practice of hunting has actually benefited nature conservation since areas of woodland have been left as 'cover' for foxes, and because foxes have not been hunted to extinction. Opponents of fox hunting argue that it is responsible for the barbaric death of particular foxes and that it promotes an exploitative, destructive attitude to wildlife. A very similar debate continues over wildfowling. Shooters maintain that they have an interest in preserving viable populations of their quarry and that they have extensive knowledge about the birds they hunt. Nature conservationists are often sceptical. Still, wildfowlers participate in nature conservation groups, even in bird counts. Moreover, the shooters' society – the Wildfowlers Association of Great Britain and Ireland – recently changed its name to the British Association for Conservation and Shooting (Nicholson 1987, p. 44), thereby signalling – depending on one's view – the society's adoption of either conservationist goals or conservationist rhetoric. Anglers have yet to face this issue on a large scale (except in the matter of lead weights, which were linked to bird deaths, in particular fatalities amongst swans) but similar problems can be anticipated for them too.

It is not my ambition in this book to adjudicate in such matters. This is not a moral or philosophical treatise, since I have no special authority in such areas on which to call.[3] Rather, my aim is to explain how a variety of social, commercial and political forces have acted to shape the agenda of the green movement, how some issues have risen to prominence while others have suffered relative neglect.

SHAPING THE MEANING OF GREEN

The factors involved in this explanation are very diverse. There are large-scale political and commercial influences. The adoption of green issues, in particular the protection of the ozone layer, by the Conservative Party has already been mentioned. A comparable action, raising the profile of green issues, has been the competition among British supermarkets to woo the green (and probably affluent) consumer. Other highly influential actions have been undertaken much less publicly. In response to increasing unease in the Western world about toxic wastes, there has developed an international trade in waste which relocates the problem into the Third World. Those responsible for safeguarding the Western world's environment in this way have been slow to seek publicity and civic gratitude for their labours.

There have also been less dramatic but possibly equally consequential actions. Television coverage of a range of environmental issues, but in particular of natural history, is believed to have played a large part in shaping public attitudes to wildlife (Nicholson 1987, pp. 78–80). Hundreds of environmental groups and campaign organizations have been active, even just within the UK, in the last fifteen years. As will be seen in Chapter 2, the fate and influence of these groups has sometimes been affected by overt political and commercial decisions, sometimes by government policy; but it has also been shaped by the local circumstance and even the personal qualities of members.

In studying the shaping of the environmental movement it is important not to restrict one's enquiries to the *actions* of players in the environmental game. One should also take account of the influence exerted by structures and institutions. In particular, it is important to examine the impact of voting systems on the development of environmental pressure groups and politics. In general, as will be seen in Chapter 3, where the electoral system operates solely on a 'first past the post' system, green parties have found it hard to establish themselves. In turn this has had implications for the vitality of environmental pressure groups. Although the electoral system is a clear example of a crucial institutional context, there are other examples, not least aspects of tax, company and charity law which have influenced the activities pressure groups have been able to undertake.

The last, and in many respects most important, question about the shape of the green movement is the extent to which the problems it identifies are treated in an international context. Much of the recent green wave has risen in Europe (but see Hays 1987); certainly it is the pressure groups, politicians, advertising agencies and media of the West who are responsible for bringing green issues to the forefront of our attention. But, as I mentioned, green issues have been very important for the democracy movements in Eastern Europe also. Equally, the practice of dumping the West's toxic waste in the Third World highlights the significance of environmental issues to developing countries and to international trading relations. It is important to assess green issues not solely with respect to their likely impact on our lives – our health, wealth and surroundings – in the West. One has to consider their impact, and the impact of the 'solutions' we propose for our own problems, on the Third World.

As we shall see in Chapter 5, the environmental problems of the Third World are severe. In the words of the United Nations report on environment and development (World Commission on Environment and Development 1987, p. 22): 'Developing countries face the obvious life-threatening challenges of desertification, deforestation, and pollution, and endure most of the poverty associated with environmental degradation.' The report (commonly termed the Brundtland Report, after the Commission's chairperson, the former Prime Minister of

Norway) makes clear the intimate connections between environmental issues and the enduring problems of poverty and lack of development. As I shall argue, a concern with the Third World's environment – far from a distraction from the economic and political needs of its people – is essential if those needs are to be properly addressed.

THE STATUS OF THE GREEN CASE

The last general issue to be taken up in this Introduction is the status or standing of green arguments. By this I do not mean the moral correctness of shooting or of the preservation of particular species; I have, as I have said, no particular authority in this matter. What I can describe, however, is the kind of appeal that the green case has for certain groups in society and the kinds of authority that green activists claim for their own arguments.

The first of these can be illustrated by the point just made about the significance of green matters to the Third World. Many on the left of politics, concerned to prioritize the alleviation of poverty and deprivation in both the First and Third Worlds, have tended to regard environmental issues as the preserve, at best, of the 'soft left'. At worst, environmentalism may be viewed as an attempt by the already wealthy to protect their own surroundings under the guise of preserving wildlife or the countryside. In this regard, as Rootes notes, left-wing parties may face a difficulty in introducing environmental protection policies that inhibit growth: 'Socialist parties [may be] hamstrung . . . they are propelled by ideological commitment and part of socialist ideology dictates that economic development is essential to the betterment of the condition of the working class' (Rootes 1990, p. 10). However, once it is shown that environmental improvements can benefit the poor, in fact that they can benefit the poor most of all, this distrust of green politics tends to disappear. After all, as Lowe and Rüdig (1986, p. 523) note, 'working-class people are usually more exposed to environmental hazards than others'. As will be seen in Chapter 5, the study of Third-World problems makes this point very clearly.

Second, there is the question of the authority claimed by green activists. An important point to which I shall return several times is the role of factual, scientifically based claims in the green case. Many social movements in this century have been based on moral or religious claims: for example, that abortion is morally wrong, that civil rights should be extended to minority populations or that God meant women to join (or be excluded from) the priesthood. While there are moral claims associated with the green case, it is also highly dependent on specifically scientific and technical considerations. In particular it depends on scientific predictions about, for instance, what would happen if we destroyed the ozone layer. I shall argue that the green case is unusually dependent on scientific authority and that this fact lends the movement peculiar weaknesses as well as strengths.

Finally, in this Introduction, is an outline of the book's contents. Chapter 1 offers an outline of the leading environmental issues as they are perceived in the 1990s. The next chapter traces the way in which the green case has come to public attention, focusing specifically on the role played by environmental organizations and pressure groups. The wider politics of the green movement in the West is the subject of Chapter 3; it examines public interest in the environment, the response of political parties and the (occasionally cynical) adaptation of industry and commerce to 'green consciousness'. This is followed by a study of the role of scientific authority in the green movement and in environmental controversies. Chapter 5 concerns the connection between environmental problems and social and economic development in the Third World. The Third World is the location of some of the most pressing environmental problems: for example, apart from those in Australia, all the world's rain forests are there. But, even in less obvious ways, the connection is still very important. Many Third-World economies depend on such extractive or primary industries as mining, logging, or farming. These have enormous environmental impacts. Also industrialization in the underdeveloped world would have huge consequences for the production of pollutants; carbon dioxide emissions and the production of ozone-unfriendly chemicals would both increase greatly. Moreover, the First World exercises a great influence over the course of Third World development. Commonly, it is either Western banks and agencies which are funding development projects or it is Western firms which are locating aspects (often environmentally 'dirty' aspects) of their business in the Third World. In this chapter I relate the environmental problems facing the Third World to these countries' position of 'dependent development', that is development under the restriction of economic weakness and debt. In the Afterword I draw together the themes of the book and examine the contribution which the social sciences can make to our understanding of environmental problems.

NOTES

1 The figure in the preceding (1984) elections had been less than a quarter of 1 per cent. A direct comparison is not a fair one, though, since the Greens did not contest all seats on the earlier occasion. See Chapter 3 for more details on the UK Green Party.
2 It is an irony worth noting that the the term 'green revolution' which is now rather commonly applied to the great change in attitude towards green issues originally applied to a technical innovation in agriculture which, while initially promising to aid Third-World economies, had many adverse consequences (see Yearley 1988, pp. 163–7). It seems to be tempting fate to apply it so soon to another apparently benign phenomenon.
3 This is not to say that I subscribe wholeheartedly to a distinction between facts and values. For example, later in the book we shall come across agencies which claim to have a certain policy but whose actions confound that policy. Such instances invite a prima-facie charge of hypocrisy. What I am keen to point out is that I will not be assessing the correctness of moral claims as much as seeking to explain why people come to adopt certain views and why it is that some views come to dominate while others come to be regarded as insupportable.

CHAPTER 1

An outline of
the issues

In the Introduction I described the recent increase in green awareness, particularly in Britain, and mentioned some of the environmental problems which have achieved the greatest public recognition. I stated then that, although there are a great many problems to which the label 'green' has been attached, there is a core of problems which most environmental activists in most countries would place on a list of pressing issues. The purpose of this chapter is to provide an overview of these. In some cases the problems have become so familiar, at least in name, that it is hard to be clear about the details. Even people who ought to know better have apparently become confused. Thus, in 1989 the British-owned car manufacturer Austin-Rover was criticized by the UK Advertising Standards Authority for running an advertising campaign suggesting that engines which burned lead-free petrol would help the problem of the diminishing ozone layer (*Guardian* 12 July 1989, p. 3). Yet lead emissions and ozone depletion are entirely unrelated problems. Austin-Rover were very far from being alone in making errors of this sort. It is all too easy for 'green issues' to become conflated. Accordingly, I shall provide some technical information which will allow the issues to be more fully appreciated. At the same time it will be possible to introduce the political and socio-economic context in which the problems have arisen; throughout the remainder of the book I shall concentrate on these political and socio-economic features.

THE 'HOLE' IN THE OZONE LAYER

Ozone is a gas which, under normal circumstances, is rarely found at ground level. Until recently, therefore, most people have had no familiarity with it unless they happen to know it is responsible for the smell associated with photocopiers. However, it is not rare for the same reason as, for example, helium is. The atmosphere contains relatively very few atoms of helium; hence, it is simply uncommon. Ozone is different. It is made up of oxygen atoms which are themselves very numerous. The gas 'oxygen' which we breathe and which comprises around one fifth of the atmosphere is composed of molecules, each made up of two oxygen atoms. Ozone is a very close chemical relative of oxygen gas but each molecule is composed of three oxygen atoms. Under certain circumstances oxygen gas (O_2) can be turned into ozone gas (O_3); in other conditions the reaction goes the opposite way.

Nearly everywhere on this planet oxygen is by far the commoner gas, the form which the atoms 'prefer' to adopt. Ozone prepared in a laboratory will normally revert to oxygen, every two molecules of the former producing three of the latter. A container of oxygen gas, on the other hand, will not generate any ozone. Chemists would describe ozone as the higher energy gas, meaning that it requires a good deal of chemical energy to turn oxygen into ozone but that, with only the slightest persuasion, ozone will revert back into oxygen. Ozone is thus a relatively unstable chemical substance. Or, to put it another way, ozone is a very reactive gas: it is so ready to turn into oxygen that it will enter into reactions with a very wide range of other chemicals.

However, high in the earth's atmosphere – between about 20 and 50 kilometres up – there is a band in which ozone is relatively plentiful. This region, part of the stratosphere, is exposed to powerful radiation coming directly from the sun. When this radiation strikes the atmosphere it imparts sufficient energy to the oxygen gas to cause some of it to be converted into ozone. Consequently, at this altitude ozone is naturally common. Of course, ozone molecules continue to revert to the more stable form but this rate of conversion is matched by the continuous creation of new ozone. The two processes long ago reached equilibrium and created a spherical band around the earth, rich in ozone.

Once this band was in place it had a marked effect upon the earth since it selectively screened out radiation, particularly high-energy ultra-violet radiation, from the sun. Life evolved under the protection of this screen. If it were removed allowing a great increase of high-energy radiation reaching the earth's surface, the consequences would be wide-ranging. Since strong ultra-violet radiation can damage the chemical structure of organic material, the effects can be expected to include an increase in the incidence of skin cancer in humans and animals, a rise in the number of mutations in plant growth and damage to plankton (important as the base of the food chain). Ultra-violet radiation also promotes the formation of chemical smogs; it may even contribute to the warming of the earth's surface.

The perceived threat to this ozone layer was one of the turning points in the political fortune of green issues. Above all, it was the one issue which was initially championed by the Conservative administration in Britain and was the focus of a very successful British consumer campaign. The well-known link, which allowed government to set policy and consumers to make a choice, is the group of chemicals known collectively as CFCs (short for chlorofluorocarbons). These are humanly-made gases, developed early this century, which were designed to be exceptionally unreactive. They are non-flammable, they do not react with common substances and are not poisonous, nor do they break down easily. They have been used extensively in industrial societies. Most notoriously, they are used as propellants in aerosol cans. Certain CFCs can be liquefied easily by pressure even at room temperatures. When the pressure is released they evaporate rapidly. This stream of evaporating gas can be used to carry along other chemicals: for example, perfumes, paints, or deodorants. Being largely unreactive, the CFCs do not interfere with the perfume or poison the user.

The CFCs have other well-known uses. The same property that makes them suitable for use in aerosols equips them to serve as the coolant in refrigerators and freezers. They can be liquefied by pressure outside the appliance, pumped into the cool chamber and then allowed to evaporate, a process which sucks in heat. Their lack of reactivity suits them for a number of other purposes: they can be used to extinguish fires by smothering the flames and can be employed to clean out sensitive electronic equipment in the sure knowledge that they will not react with the components. They can be used in the manufacture of plastic foams (for insulating materials or for hamburger containers) since they can safely be blown into molten plastics and will not endanger the users of the material; they are also popular in such products because the CFCs are themselves good insulators.

All of these things CFCs did well enough. But it was precisely their unreactiveness and their consequent long life which became a problem. Released into the atmosphere when deodorants were sprayed or when refrigerators were discarded, the CFCs persisted. They became distributed throughout the atmosphere. Those that reached as high as the ozone layer were bombarded by high-energy radiation and began to decompose. In this process they released chlorine compounds which, in turn, interacted vigorously with ozone to encourage its breakdown.

While the CFCs are dispersed throughout the whole atmosphere, the process of ozone depletion is concentrated. The profound cold in the upper atmosphere above the poles effectively isolates the polar air. It also allows extensive ice clouds to form in the polar winter. During the winter the pole is also dark; consequently, there is little chemical activity involving CFCs (*Green Magazine* December 1989, pp. 32–3). However, the ice clouds – whose surface chemistry facilitates the reaction in which ozone is decomposed – persist into the spring. So each year the first sunlight of spring causes a very rapid interaction between the chlorine compounds and the polar ozone layer. The reaction proceeds in such a way that the active chlorine is almost perpetually recreated; it is hardly used up in the reaction at all. Accordingly, the problem tends to get worse each spring. While the ozone layer is slowly thinning over all the planet, the special conditions found in the polar regions mean that there are now annual 'holes' (areas of extreme thinning) over both poles. Worse, some air invariably escapes from the polar vortices and, as the ozone depletion in the 'holes' intensifies, 'some parcels of ozone deficient atmosphere can wander for considerable distances before dispersing' (Everest 1989, p. 18). Before long this process could permit high doses of ultra-violet radiation to strike major centres of population close to the poles,[1] particularly those (say in Australia or Argentina) near the Antarctic where depletion is more advanced.

The prospects of increased rates of skin cancer and of reductions in food production are clearly alarming. And the international meetings convened since 1985 to discuss action on CFCs suggest that this alarm has prompted a concerted effort to respond to the problem. Yet it is not as though the problem were newly discovered (see the account of the controversy over CFCs in Dotto and Schiff 1978). Warnings about the effects of CFCs were first issued in the 1970s and, in the USA, their use in aerosol spray cans was progressively phased out from 1978 (Dotto and Schiff 1978, pp. 287–8). Elsewhere the potential dangers were long regarded as unproven. The first reports of a major diminution of the ozone layer in 1985 are now widely described as a turning-point. There is currently a 'Montreal Protocol on Substances that Deplete the Ozone Layer' (*Guardian* 5 May 1989, p. 25) and agreement among the signatories to phase out CFCs and halons (related substances with bromine in place of chlorine) before the year 2000. But, according to environmentalists, this action is deficient in at least two important regards.

First, there are already many tons of CFCs circulating in the atmosphere and on their way towards the ozone layer. There is also a large reservoir in domestic refrigerators, air-conditioning systems, commercial cooling systems (in warehouses and so on) and in insulating materials. In some cases, these materials can be collected after use and possibly recycled. However, even without any newly manufactured 'ozone eaters', the stock in the atmosphere is likely to continue to grow.[2] This problem is compounded by the second consideration: there are many countries that are only just beginning to wish to use CFCs on a large scale. Chinese citizens currently possess few refrigerators but the potential demand is huge. Much the same can be said of India. Just these two countries could vastly increase world demand for CFCs and could reverse any reductions which are achieved in the First and Second Worlds. Current hopes are pinned on the provision of alternatives. But if these happen to be more expensive than CFCs, the poorer nations are likely to feel that there has been a great injustice.

To summarize, the problem of the 'hole' in the ozone layer has been a dramatic and well-documented issue. The industrial nations unwittingly released a serious hazard into the environment, and its effects were not local but global. International efforts were made to co-ordinate measures to reduce the problem and, once public interest was aroused, spray can manufacturers were quick to introduce substitutes. At many levels the response has been viewed as successful and this success has been offered as a cause for optimism. Depending on one's position, it shows either that existing political and commercial systems can respond adequately to environmental problems or that the inadequacies of our political and commercial systems can sometimes be overcome by vigorous campaigning and pressure-group activity.

Other aspects of this story also mark it as typical of current environmental problems. First, the problem was identified long before concerted action was taken. Second, the identification of the problem depended on highly technical and costly scientific analysis, analysis which was difficult and open to varying inter-pretations. Third, action is likely to be taken which may stop the situation from worsening but it is extremely difficult to reverse it altogether. Fourth, there is an important Third-World dimension to the problem. The British public's avoidance of CFC-driven deodorants and perfumes may obtain a great deal of publicity; far more complex and more decisive is the response of the Chinese nation. However, there are also lessons from the atypicality of this case. While some see the international agreements about ozone depletion as representing the first of many likely victories in the fight against environmental deg-radation, the unusualness of the ozone layer problem should be recognized. Relatively speaking, it is a conspicuously simple one: a single industrial product threatens a particular natural phenomenon. If a substitute for CFCs can be found and CFC use stopped, the ozone layer will gradually restore itself. Few other environmental problems are ever that simple commercially, scientifically, or politically. The next example makes that point very clearly.

GLOBAL WARMING AND THE FATE
OF THE RAIN FORESTS

The atmosphere surrounding the early prehistoric earth probably contained very little oxygen. Early life forms – algae and primitive plants – gradually drew energy from sunlight and released oxygen into the air. The first rust deposits found in the fossil record document this atmospheric change. Only once a reasonably oxygen-rich atmosphere had been produced could air-breathing land animals appear. Subsequently an approximate balance has been preserved. Animals consume oxygen and exhale carbon dioxide. In sunlight, plants use carbon dioxide as a source of carbon for building their chemical structure, and as a by-product release oxygen. Environmentalists now believe that during the last two hundred years humans have been responsible for another change in the balance of atmospheric gases. The main worry is not that humans have multiplied and increased their oxygen consumption (although they have), not even that they have cleared so many trees (although that is an anxiety), but that they have pumped so much additional carbon dioxide into the atmosphere. By and large, they have done this by burning coal, natural gas and petroleum products.

The accumulation of carbon dioxide in the atmosphere worries environmentalists because of the gas's thermal properties. Sunlight heats the earth's surface and the atmosphere above it. But this heat is gradually dissipated out into space. Year after year the sun's heat is nearly constant so that solar heating and the loss of warmth into space are in equilibrium; consequently the average temperature of the earth has become stabilized.[3] However, some gases are much better insulators than are others: carbon dioxide is a far better insulator than most other gases in the atmosphere. So, as carbon dioxide has built up, the earth has cooled less quickly. Like the glass in a greenhouse, the carbon dioxide has retained the sun's warmth. As a result the average surface temperature of the earth has risen over the last two centuries.

This global warming, or 'greenhouse effect', is thought to have many results. Sooner or later, it will affect vegetation and agriculture; for example, the cereal growing areas of the USA may become too hot and arid for continued high harvests. It will probably affect weather systems: the climate may become more extreme. But the predicted consequence which has most powerfully grasped the public imagination is rising sea-levels (Pearce 1989, pp. 168–75).

In many popular accounts this phenomenon has been associated with the melting of polar ice-caps. The Antarctic is a large continent covered in ice, in places up to five kilometres thick. A rise in global temperatures would probably begin to melt this ice-cap and would lead to a great increase in the volume of sea water. Sea-levels around the whole globe would rise in step. On the other hand, the polar cap at the Arctic is composed solely of floating ice. Since ice is less dense than water, even if the whole ice-cap melted there would be no increase in the total volume of water. It is only where ice acts as a way of storing water on land (as in the Antarctic and in Greenland, Canada and so on) that there would be a problem. There is, however, enough land-based ice to cause a big problem.

Frightening though this prospect is, it is not the sole risk associated with global warming. At least as troubling is the possibility that warmer oceans will simply expand, rising – very slowly – like the mercury in a thermometer. The oceans might only expand by the slightest fraction but the vast volume of water they contain would translate this into an appreciable rise measured at the water's edge. Many major cities throughout the world are at ports or are close to the sea. All these would be threatened by a rise in sea-level; so too would low-lying island countries (such as the Maldives in the Indian Ocean) and low, flat countries such as Bangladesh, which is already prey to disastrous floods during the monsoon.

There now appears to be wide agreement about the reality of the greenhouse effect and about rising sea-levels (for a helpful review see Boyle and Ardill 1989, pp. 7–46). Unfortunately, it is difficult to establish how rapidly the effect is working. Historical statistics which would allow long-term comparisons are not very reliable. Equally, the ordinary fluctuations in climate and tidal levels make the trend difficult to measure and even harder to extrapolate; according to one oceanographer, 'Analyses of sea level trends need at least 20 years of measurements. There are no short cuts, no ways of speeding up the steady accretion of data' (Pugh 1989, p. 29). There are many competing estimates of just how quickly temperatures will rise and of the way that sea-level will vary with temperature. The calculations are also complicated by the finding that the oceans themselves absorb carbon dioxide, both because they dissolve it and because marine creatures use it in building their bodies (Pearce 1989, pp. 139–56). Those marine fauna and flora that sink to the sea floor as they die effectively remove carbon from the atmospheric cycle. There is considerable uncertainty about the amount which can be consumed in this way.

Carbon dioxide is regarded as the most important greenhouse gas. Every year it is produced by the billions of tonnes (that is, thousands of billions of kilograms) in industry, in power stations (burning coal, gas, or oil) and by engines. Yet it is not the sole culprit. It was mentioned earlier that CFCs are good insulators; it is therefore no surprise that they too act to retain the earth's heat. They are vastly more effective than carbon dioxide in this regard: molecule for molecule they are thousands of times as good at insulating. Accordingly, although they are much less common in the atmosphere than carbon dioxide, CFCs may contribute around 15 per cent of the greenhouse effect (*Time* 2 January 1989, p. 26). Other gases play a part too: for example, nitrogen oxides (also emitted by car engines) and methane. The latter is produced by bacteria living in cattle's digestive systems, by the trillions of termites in the world and by natural decomposition on rubbish dumps.

Although the analysis of the problem is roughly agreed the response to it is far from settled. Clearly, stopping the production of CFCs will help. But the major threat derives from continued carbon dioxide production. Developing countries can hardly hope to industrialize without increasing the amount they emit; in particular, they cannot readily proceed with electrification without burning more fossil fuels in their power stations. At an international conference, backed by the United Nations and held in The Netherlands in November 1989, government ministers were unable to reach agreement about viable policies (*The Independent* 8 November 1989, p. 16). The most radical position, preferred by many continental European nations, recommended a freeze by the year 2000 at present levels of carbon dioxide emission. The UK offered to accept a freeze but not at such a low level (although its position was subsequently relaxed (*The*

Independent 5 February 1990, p. 3)). But the USA, the Soviet
Union and, significantly, India and China stated that they could
not accept a freeze by that date.

On the same day that the report of that meeting appeared, Mrs
Thatcher was addressing the United Nations General Assembly
in New York. She identified accumulation of carbon dioxide in
the atmosphere as one of the central problems facing humankind.[4] Her approach was to insist that 'Before we act, we need
the best possible scientific assessment' (*Guardian* 9 November
1989, p. 7). She announced that the UK was to establish 'a
new centre for the prediction of climate change'. Critical voices
were soon raised, insisting that some steps had to be taken to
restrict the growth of atmospheric carbon dioxide even while
such research was being conducted.

In her speech, the UK's Prime Minister did make one proposal
to combat the greenhouse effect; she advocated the increased
use of nuclear power generation, one of the ways of producing
electricity which yields no carbon dioxide. As will be described
below, many people have objections to the use of nuclear power.
Nevertheless, other ways of producing electricity without carbon
dioxide are probably limited. Tidal power, wind power, solar
heating and hydro-electric generation are all likely to be of
restricted applicability, although it should be acknowledged that
much work remains to be done on their development and that
studies of alternative energy have received few funds in comparison with the investment in nuclear research. Among environmentalists, the most widely accepted policy recommendations
currently centre on ways of using energy more effectively. For
example, if people can be persuaded to share transport, this
cuts carbon dioxide emissions without reducing their ability to
travel. Similarly, if power stations can be made more efficient
in turning, say, coal's energy into electricity we will reduce our
contribution to the greenhouse effect without having to economize on electricity. Again, if we insulate our houses and factories
better, we will use less electricity in staying warm. If widely
adopted, such measures would slow the increase in the release
of carbon dioxide; if pursued very systematically they might
even decrease our output of the gas. However, no one expects
any such measures to reduce our output to pre-industrial levels.
Consequently, all we can anticipate is further global warming.

Only one process is known to absorb carbon dioxide on a large scale: plant photosynthesis.[5] As mentioned above, green plants develop by extracting carbon from this gas. The bulk of the weight of any tree, plant, or blade of grass is composed of carbon derived in this manner. The bigger the plant the more carbon it incorporates. This implies that vast programmes of forest planting would directly combat the greenhouse effect. Unfortunately, as has been well publicized, quite the opposite has been happening in the last decade. The world's most prolific forests, the tropical rain forests, are being cut down and not replanted. Worse still, they are not even always being felled for timber, a use which keeps the carbon locked up in the wood. They are often cleared to provide agricultural land. The easiest method of clearance is adopted; trees are simply being burned, turning their carbon back into carbon dioxide. In this way, the destruction of the rain forests is contributing to global warming. One estimate puts the amount of carbon added to the atmosphere in this way at around one billion tonnes each year, about one sixth of the total amount of carbon added (Schoon and Wilkie 1988, p. 17).

As their name suggests, the tropical rain forests are located around the globe in a band between the Tropic of Cancer (which passes through Mexico, the Sahara and India) and, to the south, the Tropic of Capricorn (passing through Argentina, Namibia and Australia). Where conditions were moist enough rain forests developed; they are still extensive in west central Africa (for example in Gabon, Cameroon and Zaïre), in the Amazon region, in eastern parts of Central America (for example, Nicaragua, Costa Rica and Belize) and in South-East Asia (for instance, in Burma, Malaysia, Indonesia, Vietnam and Papua New Guinea) (see Gradwohl and Greenberg 1988, pp. 25–51).

The background to the destruction of forests in these areas is not uniform. The trees of eastern Malaysia are currently being felled for use by Japanese industry: according to one report, over two thirds of Japanese timber imports are supplied from that one area (Appleton 1989, p. 505). Some of this wood has even been used for pulping, a process for which softwoods are just as well suited. European timber sources lie chiefly in Africa, particularly in Gabon and Liberia. These two timber trades both considerably exceed the amount of timber exported from South and Central America (primarily to North America). Yet it is the forests of the Amazon, being cleared for agriculture or mining, which have attained the greatest notoriety. This is because dramatic photographs of burning rain forest have been given wide publicity in the developed world. These arresting images have come to symbolize the heedlessness of much environmental destruction.

Developments in the Amazonian rain forest are extremely complex (see Hecht and Cockburn 1989a, 1989b). In Brazil, for example, traditional forest dwellers, national politicians, foreign firms, foreign banks, foreign conservationists, wealthy local ranchers, and international aid agencies have all had a hand in determining the fate of the forests. This story has so comprehensive a cast that it can usefully stand as a paradigm for the environmental problems of the Third World. These issues will be examined in detail in Chapter 5, but the bare bones of the matter are as follows.

Brazil faces an enormous debt to foreign, largely US, banks. At the same time, much of the population is extremely poor.[6] The poor exert pressure on the authorities to make more land available to them. Yet ownership of highly productive agricultural land is concentrated in the hands of wealthy ranchers and some foreign firms. They are able to produce food crops for export and justify their opposition to land redistribution on the grounds that their exports service the debt. 'Colonization' of the rain forest appears to offer a solution to both problems. If the forest is cleared, the poor can be given new land and the ranchers can keep their farms. Indeed, they too can have some of the former forest.

Although the figures are disputed (see the *Guardian* 7 April 1989, p. 14), it is plain that forest clearance has been proceeding rapidly; in the Amazonian region alone, an area of forest about the size of England can be cleared in a single year. But demand for land is not easily satisfied. For one thing, the poor are very poor and the population is growing. Equally, as Latin American countries' huge debts are not easily met, it is tempting to take more and more land to increase the amount of produce for export. Most notoriously, rain forests have been cleared to enable cattle to be reared whose meat is exported for use in hamburgers and other fast foods. Most publicity was attracted to this practice in Central America, notably in Costa Rica, where, according to one estimate, 'It takes 55 square feet of rain forest to raise enough beef to make a single American hamburger' (*The Sunday Times Magazine* 26 February 1989, p. 37). More disturbingly, the rain forests are ideally suited to local conditions whereas arable farming and grazing are commonly unsuitable. The forests are enormously productive in their use of sunlight, while their biological richness allows them to soak up the prodigious rainfall. Moreover, their great productivity means that they quickly deposit organic matter and build up a soil. If the forests are removed the heavy rains tend to run off immediately, removing the soil. Without the life cycle of the forest the soil is not replenished. Consequently, the initially rich land soon degrades. Within a few years the dense, highly productive forest growing on shallow but rich soil can be replaced with an eroded landscape poorly suited to any form of agriculture. Once this has happened the obvious temptation is to clear a further patch of forest.

There are three further victims of this colonization to which attention should be drawn. These victims suffer not only in the Amazon but anywhere that rain forest clearance takes place. The first is the climate. We have seen that the forest acts as a 'sponge', preventing the heavy rains from being too erosive. But the forest sponge also keeps the immediate atmosphere moist and therefore cooler. Removal of the forest thus threatens to make the climate more severe. The more that is removed, the greater this effect will be. Second of the victims are the traditional peoples of the forest. Destruction of the forest takes away the basis of their economy. Commonly, their 'rights' to the forest are not enshrined in modern law and they are not regarded as the forest's owners. Their interests receive little legal protection. One may accept that such groups have to surrender some of the forest to the greater national interest but the forests are all too often occupied without any attempt to accommodate these people's needs. Finally, there are other biological victims: birds and animals that are restricted to the forests and the plants of the forests themselves. This threat to species will be considered in the next section.

In summary, the problems of global warming and of rain forest destruction show some similarities to the question of ozone depletion. The problem is international, tied to sophisticated scientific issues and hard to reverse. Yet the commercial and political linkages in this case are much more complex and much harder to address than in the previous example. The West can stop producing and releasing CFCs, but it will not restore the forest cover in Europe, North America or Japan, which was long ago destroyed. For their part, developing countries may be able to adopt alternatives to CFCs but they have little choice but to continue releasing large volumes of carbon dioxide.

THE LOSS OF HABITATS AND THE EXTINCTION OF SPECIES

People have long been fascinated by rare and unusual species; early modern Europe was thrilled by the importing of exotic animals and plants. We have also known for a long time that humans can eliminate whole populations of animals, whether by design (as with wolves in Britain and Ireland) or by heedless killing (as with the North American passenger pigeon and, very nearly, the bison). Efforts to conserve endangered creatures are familiar from at least the nineteenth century. Early conservation activities tended to be directed at particular species. For example, the origins of the Royal Society for the Protection of Birds (RSPB) lie in a movement which aimed to protect those birds threatened by the fashion trade in feathers (see Hammond 1983, p. 158 and the account in Chapter 2). In many cases this emphasis has continued, particularly for species which appeal strongly to people. Pandas, with their apparent reluctance to breed, have made international news. Great public concern has been stirred about the culling of seals and about the whaling industry. But the emphasis amongst wildlife conservationists has shifted in the last twenty years away from a concern about species to an interest in habitats. It may be possible to protect birds from hunters, but if the forests or the estuaries in which they live are destroyed this will harm the birds just as comprehensively as ever the hunters could. Even though the individual responsibility of the hunter is clearer, habitat destruction tends to be rather more damaging to a species than hunting.

Wildlife conservation organizations have a long and mostly venerable history. In the UK, the largest environmental organization, the Royal Society for the Protection of Birds is explicitly concerned with wildlife (largely native wildlife) conservation. The Royal Society for Nature Conservation was, until very recently, the second largest such group.[7] In Chapter 2 we will examine how they have responded to the broadening of environmental concerns and to the growing internationalism of ecological problems. But at this stage it is sufficient to observe that they have followed the progression from species to habitats. In particular, both organizations have noted that the biggest threats to British wildlife have come not from collectors or hunters but from changing agricultural practices. Since the 1950s the countryside has been transformed. Typically, hedges have been cleared; what remained of old forests has dwindled, to be replaced, if at all, with uniform plantings of imported conifers; small fields have been merged into 'prairies' planted with a single crop, the weeds and pests controlled by large doses of agro-chemicals; even grasslands have been re-sown with newer, non-native varieties of grass from which wildflowers have been excluded (Moore 1987, pp. 25–66; Newby 1988, pp. 5–29 and 87–111; Seddon 1989, pp. 89–114). All these developments have rendered the countryside far less able to support wildlife although, in the late 1980s, some success was achieved in reversing the policies which had encouraged these developments (Newby 1988, pp. 106–11). Conservation groups have pressed for changes in agricultural policy and have tried to acquire, or persuade the government to acquire, large reserves on which traditional habitats can be maintained. In the RSPB's case, they face an additional problem since many 'British' birds are migratory and spend large parts of the year elsewhere. There is little value in protecting British habitats if the birds' other haunts, or even feeding points along the migration path, are being destroyed. This organization has thus been led increasingly into international conservation activities.

The same concern with habitat maintenance is prevalent throughout the West and has influenced the West's approach to conservation activities elsewhere in the world. The rain forests are now the prime example of an endangered habitat and a great many Western conservation groups are campaigning and fund-raising on their behalf. In this case, as we have already seen, there are additional reasons for wishing to preserve the forests since they represent a massive stock of organic carbon.

At the same time, the rain forests are extraordinarily rich in species. An argument for their protection can be made in terms of the inherent value of the unique creatures and plants they contain. This appeal can also be made more pragmatic by pointing out that these species form a colossal 'bank' of genetic material, much of which has never been investigated (for a review see R. and C. Prescott-Allen 1988). It can be argued that the plants of the rain forest, which already offer medically and industrially important chemicals, will afford further medicines, new raw materials for industry and genetic materials important to agricultural biotechnology.[8] The wide variety of arguments available illustrates an important point. As we will see in Chapters 2 and 3, there are a great many reasons for people's involvement in conservation. People's responses to the fate of attractive seals and majestic whales probably have little in common with their feelings about obscure plants or rare earwigs.[9] In the course of fund-raising and lobbying, conservation organizations have sought to draw on the whole range of possible motivations for defending the environment. Finding a sound commercial and impersonal reason for conserving the rain forests (for example, the industrial value of their genetic stock) is a powerful rationale even if it is not the conservationists' own motivation for protecting them.

So far we have seen that the conservation of species can be undertaken for the animals' and plants' sake or because of the products which may be derived from them. But the reasons for, and the context of, conservation may be more complex. Some indication of the politics of conservation work can be gleaned from the case of elephants in the Tsavo National Park of south-eastern Kenya (Jackman 1989).

With the rising price of ivory and the persistent poverty in many Third-World countries, it has become increasingly attractive to some people to kill elephants for their tusks. The death of large numbers of elephants, simply for their tusks (their bodies are left to decay and to be scavenged) has excited the concern of conservationists and large numbers of the public; in 1989 it was prominent news in Africa and Europe.

Such hunting is not wholly new; from the Tsavo Park's establishment in 1948 there had been some poaching of elephants, their tusks being sold to international dealers. But this early hunting had been carried out by local tribes, taking limited numbers with poisoned arrows. The herds could survive this level of hunting and, despite a prolonged drought, the park's elephant population stood at nearly 17,500 in 1972. Sixteen years later, it was down to a quarter of this size. They had suffered sustained assaults from poachers using vehicles to cover the terrain quickly and armed with automatic weapons. The gangs appeared quite ruthless in their hunting. They had armed themselves with advanced weapons available from the war in Somalia (*International Herald Tribune* 29 January 1990, p. 4); in fact, according to Jackman, some of the hunters 'are ethnic Somalis with Kenyan nationality but many are from Somalia itself, including army deserters' (1989, p. 58). The park staff have been reorganized and now adopt a paramilitary style themselves, supported by spotter planes. The plight of the elephants has stirred considerable international sympathy; the herds could easily be hunted to extinction. The escalating human violence causes anxiety too; both warders and poachers are often killed. But two other features make this story especially complex.

The first is the impact of this remorseless hunting on the Kenyan economy. The country is extremely reliant on wildlife-based tourism. While individuals no doubt benefit from the illicit ivory business and there are even fears that some people who work on the reserves accept bribes to assist the poachers, the trade is injurious to the country's economy. This is perhaps the most unsentimental reason for valuing one's wildlife. But in this case the reasoning takes a further twist for there are suggestions that the Kenyan state's enemies encourage the economic misery which poaching will bring. As Jackman puts it, 'Kenyans are now wondering if the slaughter of their elephants is a deliberate attempt by the Somalis to destabilize the country' (1989, p. 58). On this view, wildlife destruction may not even be attributable to the greed or desperation of individual poachers. It may be one move in a Machiavellian political strategy.

The second point which Jackman raises is that the elephants are important not just in their own right, nor even for their touristic appeal but because they are central to the maintenance of the ecosystem:

> They open up the dense Commiphora thorn thickets, allowing grasslands to spring up where herds of oryx, impala, zebras and antelope may graze.
>
> As the grasslands spread, the water table rises, with the roots of the perennial grasses reaching down 20 feet and more to break up the hard pan created by permanent scrub. . . . [W]herever they roam, their tusking and mud-wallowing create waterholes where other animals can drink.
>
> Now, with the elephants' demise, the scrub is returning, and with it the tsetse fly – killer of cattle. Seasonal streams are drying up. Waterholes are disappearing (Jackman 1989, p. 59).

This example implies that threats to species do not even stop at that one species but have implications for diverse aspects of the surrounding environment. Wildlife conservation may often be necessary to general ecological protection.

Overall we may now conclude that species and habitat conservation are well under way, although the growing appreciation of the threats is not, by itself, sufficient to halt them. There are many reasons for conserving species and habitats, some personal and emotional, and some, such as the link between rain forest plants and medicines, rooted in self-interest. But an understanding of these threats also needs to encompass the economic and political context. That context may include the agricultural policy of the First World: for example, Europe's Common Agricultural Policy, which has encouraged the development of intensive farming. It may be Third-World debt and poverty that has encouraged the short-term exploitation of rain forests. Finally, it may be explicit politics which leads wildlife to be seen as an enemy's economic resource, to be undermined whenever possible.

THREATS TO FOOD AND WATER

Since the late 1950s, when wartime restrictions were finally fully lifted, the developed world has experienced a period of food abundance. Although the details of the story differ from one country to another, food production has become big business. Throughout the Western world, farming has become much more commercially efficient; it has become dependent on scientific innovations in agricultural practice; and control over it has generally passed into the hands of large companies, known as agribusinesses (see George 1977, pp. 158–91 and Newby 1980, pp. 108–19).

The last thirty years have witnessed a transformation in what we eat and in the way it is produced. Taking the case of Britain, our diet has become much more diverse and almost entirely freed from dependence on seasonal crops. We have allowed businesses to take a large role in food preparation, so much so that by the 'beginning of the 1980s, 70 per cent of the British diet comprised processed foods' (London Food Commission 1989, p. 1). The food itself has also changed a great deal, with animals and crops selected with an eye to the producers' and processors' requirements (for examples see Seddon 1989, pp. 160, 165 and 193). Furthermore, the trend has been for livestock to be kept as economically as possible, often crowded close together. They have been dosed with antibiotics, in many cases to encourage them to grow quickly as well as to combat the infections promoted by their confinement (Brunner 1988).

For their part, foodcrops have been extensively treated with chemical fertilizers, weed killers and pest and disease control agents. The foodstuffs into which these products are converted may contain added synthetic colours, flavourings and preservatives (for an overview see Millstone 1986). Many processed foods contain large quantities of sugar and vegetable fats, items which consumers may otherwise be trying to exclude from their diets. It is now well known that processed meat products such as pies, sausages and burgers may contain relatively little meat; less widely publicized is the fact that even 'meats', such as ham, may contain less than three-quarters of their weight in meat (London Food Commission 1989, p. 3). Even the notion of 'meat' itself may not correspond closely with our everyday understanding of the term. Any edible, meaty part of the animal is likely to be used in processed foods. Brunner (1988) reports the case from 1980 of a group of babies in Milan who, regardless of sex, displayed premature feminization. This effect was traced to a processed baby food containing calves' ears. Some of the babyfood contained meat from around the site where the calves had received hormone injections; it still contained strong concentrations of a sex hormone.

Several of these issues have lately become matters of public concern. Yet the connection between them and environmental questions may not be immediately clear. In fact, though, the connections are numerous. First there is the impact of agricultural intensification. As described in the last section, the increased uniformity of the countryside which came about between the end of the 1950s and the 1980s threatened much of Britain's wildlife. In part, this was due simply to habitat loss. But the early and extensive use of highly toxic pesticides (such as DDT and dieldrin) also had far-reaching effects. Larger mammals and birds of prey ate the smaller birds or mammals which lived off the insects against whom the pesticides had been targeted. The toxins concentrated in the bodies of these birds and mammals at the top of the food chain. It was for this reason that peregrines nearly became extinct in Great Britain in the 1960s (Moore 1987, pp. 174–7). Foxes too died in large numbers and, as Moore ruefully notes, 'It was particularly fortunate that one of the first casualties of the persistent organochlorine insecticides was an animal whose welfare was so dear to the Establishment of the United Kingdom' (1987, p. 160). Recently, more specific pesticides have been developed which are intended to be lethal only to their target and which can be used in small quantities. But environmentalists insist that wildlife still suffers from farming practices.

Another direct connection is the way in which livestock are treated. It can easily appear hypocritical for people in the West to claim great concern about the fate of the panda or the tiger while they allow farm animals to be treated in an uncaring way. The plights of battery chickens and veal-yielding calves have attracted much public attention. A concern for the world's genetic resources is also part of this question. Just as there may be sound commercial and medical reasons for conserving forest plants, there may well be good agricultural reasons for preserving uncommon varieties of crops or livestock. Agricultural produce is now highly standardized. Commercial pressures have forced farmers to seek the same qualities in their animals: that they be fast growing or high yielding and that they be suitable for the processing industry. Once-popular strains of livestock which lack these features are in danger of dying out, although their cause is championed by organizations such as the Rare Breeds Survival Trust. Such breeds may hold valuable genetic resources (R. and C. Prescott-Allen 1988, pp. 43–7).

In the context of Third-World countries this issue becomes even more acute. The genetic richness of the world's tropical regions means that they tend to have been the source of humankind's principal foodstuffs. The ancestors of some of our most successful staple crops derive from there and great natural diversity persists (R. and C. Prescott-Allen 1988, pp. 71–82). However, the Western-led modernization of Third-World agriculture has promoted the replacement of traditional varieties by modern strains. Even where this process has yielded benefits – and that has not been universally the case (for short accounts see Lappé and Collins 1982, pp. 99–118 and Yearley 1988, pp. 163–7) – plants of potential agricultural value are becoming extinct.

Elsewhere in the Third World, particularly in the northern half of Africa and in the Middle East and Asia Minor, Central Asia, dry western areas of South America and south-west Africa, the threat of desertification has linked environmental problems with grave concerns over food (Dixon, James and Sherman 1989, p. 10). In essence, the problems arise because dryland areas have a very delicate ecology. Although the precise details vary from region to region, the danger is that overgrazing or ill-advised attempts to cultivate the land will result in a degenerative spiral. Initial efforts at increasing productivity, whether because of a growing population or because of a need to raise beef for trade (in, for example, Nigeria and the Ivory Coast (see Dixon, James and Sherman 1989, p. 29)), lead to a degradation of the soil and the gradual disappearance of protective vegetation. These are commonly followed by a diminution in the ecosystem's ability to store moisture, a further decrease in vegetation, and increased erosion, both by the wind and by run-off after rainfall. This process is difficult to reverse. It can lead to a rapid reduction in the land available for food production, great hardship for people whose traditional economy has collapsed and, in the event of a drought, to widespread famine. Although the severest problems are relatively confined, a broader definition of drylands – all of which face threats from these processes – would include 'a third of the Earth's land area, supporting 850 million people' (*Green Magazine* December 1989, p. 19).

Finally, though, it is not these direct connections between food production and ecological problems which have been the most important links. Rather, food issues have become closely associated with the green movement because they have been used to indicate that we cannot insulate ourselves from our treatment of the environment. In the UK, 1989 was the year in which 'food scares' repeatedly made headline news. For example, in the interests of economy, many battery chickens' diets were partly made up of the remains of killed birds. This had the effect of spreading bacterial infections through the flocks. Unsound practices in slaughterhouses contributed to the problem (London Food Commission 1989, p. 3). Other stories concerned toxic residues in cereals (*Guardian* 13 March 1989, p. 1), listeria in soft cheeses (*The Observer* 10 September 1989, p. 9) and cows' milk containing lead which arose from contaminated, imported feedstuffs (*Guardian* 10 November 1989, p. 10).

One current case probably represents the problems better than any other: the cattle disease bovine spongiform encephalopathy (BSE). Otherwise known as 'mad cow disease', BSE is a disease of the cow's central nervous system, and was first identified in 1985. To date, it is restricted to Great Britain and Ireland. It is believed to be closely related to the degenerative sheep disease, scrapie, which has been known for at least two hundred years. Crucially, the cattle disease may have originated in infected sheep meat being used to make a high-protein cattle feed (see Erlichman 1988 and Ferriman 1989). The danger that commentators now fear is that the disease, having leaped from one species to another through ingestion, could pass to beef-eating humans. Even after the disease was recognized, any portion of the animal that could be eaten was available for use as meat. And, given – as Williams points out (1989) – that little is understood about the operation of such diseases, the fear cannot easily be dismissed. Subsequently – from November 1989 (*Guardian* 29 January 1990, p. 3) – blanket restrictions were placed on the human consumption of those parts of cattle thought to contain the disease, these being withdrawn from sale for human consumption.[10] Still, although the direct food route along which the disease is reckoned to have passed has been abandoned, related high-protein feeds are still in use for pigs and chickens (genetically distant animals) and the material is still available for export, protected only by a warning about animals to which it should not be fed. From the consumers' point of view the compensation scheme available to farmers provoked anxiety. Although farmers were directed to destroy infected animals and were compensated for not selling them on, the amount given initially stood at only 50 per cent of the cattle's value, since the animals were officially regarded as sick. There was clearly a temptation to pass infected carcasses off as healthy ones in order to double their value (Erlichman 1988).

While BSE hints at the way in which our intervention in the natural world can rebound on us, food is not the only route for this 'feedback'. We consume our environment also by drinking it. Water quality can be dramatically affected by industrial effluents, by sewage or by waste from farms, in particular slurry (concentrated animal waste). Environmentalists also express concern about more subtle but widespread threats to water purity.

In a survey of water suppliers in England and Wales published by Friends of the Earth (UK) and the *Observer Magazine* (6 August 1989, pp. 16–24) it was found that several contaminants exceeded European Community levels at the time of the test in a number of locations. In particular, aluminium was markedly present in much of Wales, and the south-west and north-west of England. In some places aluminium is naturally present in relatively high concentrations; in others it is added by the water authorities to make the water clearer. Aluminium is thought to be related to certain forms of dementia. A second potential problem, this time occurring mainly in East Anglia, eastern England and the Welsh borders, is the presence of nitrate. Nitrate is a component of many agricultural chemicals and is itself composed of nitrogen and oxygen. It can accumulate in water supplies because of agricultural practices, in particular the large-scale application of nitrogen fertilizers. Nitrate is held to be associated with a blood disease suffered by babies (methaemoglobinaemia, known in extreme form as 'blue baby syndrome'); other risks are also claimed (see Walters 1986).

It should be noted that in both these cases it is a chemical which people are introducing into the water supply (deliberately or not) that is posing the possible health threat. The debate about water quality attained a special significance in Britain in 1989 because of the government's privatization of the water authorities in England and Wales. Opponents of privatization have argued that companies whose interest is in making a profit out of water supply will be less concerned with water purity than would a public service. Supporters of the policy reply that legal regulations can control the companies' behaviour and that official agencies are usually more strict in their policing of private companies than of state bureaucracies. Either way, this political debate has ensured that environmental considerations are brought into the limelight.

WASTE AND WASTE DISPOSAL

While all societies produce waste, modern urban societies generate it on an unprecedented scale. According to *Time* magazine (2 January 1989, p. 31), US citizens each year throw away 'two billion razors and blades and 220 million tyres. They discard enough aluminum to rebuild the entire US commercial airline fleet every three months.' In the developed world most waste is disposed of in landfill sites; it is either buried or dumped in former quarries. But space is running out, even while the volume of waste is increasing. Worse still, even plain domestic refuse may be unsafe: 'corrosive acids, long-lived organic materials and discarded metals [can] leach out of landfills into groundwater supplies, contaminating drinking water and polluting farmland' (*Time* 2 January 1989, p. 30). Industrial waste poses even more difficult problems, as does refuse from hospitals and certain farm wastes. Though the last of these is composed only of organic matter, the waste from intensive farms is so concentrated that it does not break down easily.

Countries also dispose of their waste, particularly human sewage, at sea. Many coastal towns around the UK simply discharge untreated sewage down pipes into the sea while, in other cases, the waste is treated but the resulting sludge is taken out by boats (colloquially known as 'bovril boats') and dumped offshore (Elsworth 1990, pp. 240–3). Some waste is incinerated at sea before being dumped. Nuclear waste used to be sealed in metal or concrete containers and dropped into deep areas of the sea (1990, p. 299).

One way to avoid dumping is to burn waste. This has the virtue that incinerators can be used to generate electricity or to heat water but burning inevitably yields carbon dioxide, and other noxious gases can be produced unless the combustion is very carefully monitored. Furthermore, it produces ash which still needs to be dumped somewhere. Owing to the chemical reactions which occur during burning, incinerator ash can contain an even greater concentration of dangerous substances than the original waste.

Environmentalists tend to have two responses to this problem. The first is to encourage recycling and re-use. If waste can be sorted, in the home and in industry, a high percentage of it can be used again. Glass, paper, metals and many plastics can be handled in this way. This practice is already widely adopted in continental Europe and Japan and the UK has committed itself to greatly increased recycling by the year 2000. However, demand for recycled products must coincide with supply; in autumn 1989 Britain suffered a 'mountain' of low grade waste paper because supply outstripped demand (Walker 1989, p. 13). The second response is to try to minimize unnecessary waste, for example by reducing the amount of packaging around goods and by encouraging people to buy in bulk.

Like the food issues, this question makes us aware of the way in which the quality of human life is linked to the environment. All the time that rubbish is dumped on unsightly areas well away from the majority of influential people, it does not seem like a problem. But if it starts to re-appear in groundwater or in higher charges for local services, the connection is perceived.

Perhaps the most graphic example of this attitude is the international trade in waste. As pressure groups, politicians and the citizenry in developed countries have become more concerned about the possible dangers associated with toxic waste materials, the regulations governing disposal have become more severe and are more strictly applied. The costs of disposal

have accordingly risen. It is now tempting for waste disposal
companies in the First World to seek out dumping sites in the
Third World. In part this is simply a matter of price: 'In Europe
it can cost up to $500 dollars a ton to dispose of [toxic chemical
waste]; in Africa it can cost as little as $2.50 a ton' (Dowden
1988). Poor countries, anxious to earn foreign currency any way
they can, may be willing to take the risk of burying toxic waste
on their soil. Large deals of this sort may offer impoverished,
small countries the chance nearly to double their annual national
incomes. Secrett (1988) and Dowden (1988) cite many West
African countries involved in this practice, including Guinea,
Guinea-Bissau and the Congo. According to Secrett, Benin has
also accepted radioactive waste from France.[11]

Other considerations combine with the straightforward monetary motive. Third-World countries may not have the legislation to control hazardous dumping since they generally do
not produce much waste themselves. First-World contractors
who organize disposal in the underdeveloped world are not
therefore breaking the law in a formal sense. Even when poor
countries wish to resist the waste trade, low-paid officials may
be bribed. Finally, waste disposal contractors may simply deceive
the importing country. Two investigative journalists from *The
Sunday Times* found one British company chief who

> offered to get rid of [toxic] chemicals for [a] comparatively
> cheap price ... and said the cargo, to be falsely labelled as
> liquid fertilizer, should be delivered to Newcastle-upon-Tyne,
> from where his ship would take it to Africa. (Palmer and
> Mahmood 1988)

On 22 March 1989 an international convention governing the
trade in toxic wastes was agreed in association with the United
Nations Environment Programme. But this convention neither
sought to ban the export trade in waste from the First to the
Third World nor specified how countries should trade with
non-signatory nations. A provision was suggested which would
have meant that countries could only export to other nations
whose disposal standards were at least as high as their own.
But this clause was finally dropped (*Guardian* 23 March 1989,
p. 26). Thus, the developed world can continue to send its

waste to poorer countries that maintain lower standards; the rich can impose risks on poorer countries which they deem to be unacceptable at home.

Finally, there is a danger that toxic waste does not even reach an importing country; it may just be dumped at sea. The majority of trade in waste is carried on between developed nations. But during 1988 and 1989 there were a number of cargoes which no one was willing to accept. According to *Time* magazine (2 January 1989, p. 30) one cargo of toxic incinerator ash was at sea for over two years. The fear is that companies will finally extricate themselves from this embarrassment by 'losing' the cargo at sea. According to a report in *Green Magazine* (Parker 1989) this practice is common. The article cites a researcher from the (UK) National Union of Seamen (Parker 1989, p. 22): 'A large multi-national [company] would be too fly to charter a ship and dump [the waste] themselves. There are in existence people called waste brokers who arrange things on someone else's behalf.' Deals of this sort clearly require people who will deliberately violate the law. Given the disparity between the price of disposal in the developed world and the negligible costs of dumping at sea, this illegal trade is very profitable (for an overview see Gourlay 1988). Highly paid illegal activities have always been attractive to organized crime; illicit dumping is bound to appeal too.

The final twist is that, among the substances dumped at sea, are PCBs (polychlorinated biphenyls). These chemicals, used extensively in the electrical industry (for example in industrial transformers), are difficult to dispose of, persistent and highly toxic. According to an earlier report in the same journal (*Green Magazine* October 1989, pp. 18–21), PCBs are found increasingly often in marine fish, so much so that it may soon become dangerous to eat them. In part this development is attributed to ocean dumping. It would indeed be ironic if our waste disposal practices poisoned the fish to which people have recently turned for a 'healthier' diet.

EXHAUST FUMES FROM VEHICLES

According to a recent report in *New Consumer* magazine (Issue 1 Autumn 1989, p. 26), 'cars are certainly the biggest single

The green case

consumer of world resources'. The rise of the motor industry has been almost synonymous with economic growth in the developed world this century. From the point of view of many environmentalists, cars are a key issue because, of all the major sources of pollution, they are probably the one most directly under the control of individuals. A great deal of environmentally significant change can come about if people can be persuaded to alter their motoring behaviour.

In the UK, the leading issue of the late 1980s was the use of lead-free petrol. Lead was initially added to petrol early in the twentieth century to prolong the life of engine exhaust valves; without lead, the explosive reaction in the engine wore the valves away. Sadly, the lead compound which was formed and pumped out of the exhaust (tetraethyl lead) was found, in certain concentrations, to be injurious to brain development in children. Increasingly many engines no longer need the protective effects of lead and sales of lead-free petrol have risen steadily, in large part because the government imposes a lower tax on unleaded fuel. As with the case of CFCs and the ozone layer, the use of unleaded fuel has the benefits of straightforwardness. The message and the remedy are simple. The BBC's 'pop' channel, Radio 1, was able to run a campaign encouraging its listeners to switch to lead-free. At the same time petrol companies and car manufacturers could promote sales of their product while seeming to benefit the environment because they were now lead-free. As we saw at the very beginning of this chapter, some companies even made rather extravagant claims about the good they were doing. Despite a certain air of self-congratulation which has surrounded this switch to lead-free petrol, there is a suggestion that – at least in the UK – petrol companies are replacing the lead with benzene rather than with the more expensive additive MTBE (methyl tertiary butyl ether) employed in the USA and in parts of continental Europe (*Green Magazine* December 1989, p. 73). Benzene can cause cancer.

However, lead is not the sole pollutant associated with exhaust fumes. In addition they contain oxides of nitrogen (mentioned already in the context of global warming and smogs), carbon monoxide (a highly poisonous gas present in very low concentrations), unburned fuel gases (known as 'hydrocarbons' and linked with cancer) and carbon dioxide (not toxic, but as we have seen, a 'greenhouse' gas). The first three of these, the toxic substances, can all be reduced if vehicles are fitted with a 'catalytic converter', a component of the exhaust system which results in the thorough breakdown of these gases. Catalytic converters can only work if the vehicle uses lead-free petrol, otherwise the lead damages the chemical catalysts in the converter. Even when fitted with a converter, cars continue to produce carbon dioxide. However modified, petrol-driven cars contribute to the greenhouse effect.

As in the other cases described above, there are significant international differences. Catalytic converters are routine in the USA, being necessary to meet emission standards set in 1983; Europe lags behind in this practice. The disparity was cleverly, if somewhat notoriously, exploited by Greenpeace in their poster campaign of 1988. Adopting Ford's own slogan of 'Ford gives you more', Greenpeace's posters proclaimed that 'A Ford in Britain pumps out 100 per cent more toxic fumes than a Ford back home in America'. The dramatic poster bearing this legend was not widely seen, however, possibly because advertisers were anxious about losing Ford's business (*Guardian* 27 October 1988, p. 5).

Concern about the pollution caused by petrol engines has also led to the championing of alternative fuels. In the developed world diesel has been foremost amongst these. Since it contains no lead, makers of diesel-engined cars have been quick to label it a 'green' fuel. But the UK's Advertising Standards Authority reprimanded one such manufacturer, Citroen, for praising diesel uncritically; the authority stated that 'fumes from diesel engines contain many other pollutants' (*Guardian* 12 July 1989, p. 3). The debate about the comparative virtues of petrol and diesel continues (see *New Consumer* magazine 1989, p. 27). Diesel engines tend to be more economical on fuel and thus produce less carbon dioxide per kilometre. But diesel exhaust fumes contain very fine particles of carbon which would get burned off in petrol engines. These 'particulates' contribute to smog and may have adverse health effects.

Outside the developed world other fuels are proving attractive. The purchase of oil has long been a severe drain on the world's poorer economies, so nations like Brazil have had a double incentive to turn away from petrol. One attractive option has been to develop alcohol fuels. Petrol engines can, with only slight modifications, run on alcohol. Methanol (a simple alcohol) even yields a little less carbon dioxide and fewer other pollutants than petrol, although it powers the vehicle fewer kilometres per litre. Most important though, is the fact that ethanol and methanol can be produced from agricultural sources, for example, from sugar, and are thus renewable sources of fuel. For a tropical country it also offers a degree of fuel independence. Furthermore, fuels produced from agricultural sources do not lead to an increase in atmospheric carbon dioxide; the sugar cane initially took an amount of carbon from the air and it is simply released as the fuel is burnt.

Other attractive fuel options include electrical power (even though electricity generation itself usually yields carbon dioxide) and hydrogen. Hydrogen can be produced from water, again using electrical power. When burned, the hydrogen simply re-converts into water. Both BMW and Mercedes-Benz are developing hydrogen-powered cars (*The Observer* 6 August 1989, p. 47). Ironically, hydrogen fuel may be most easily and benignly available in tropical countries where electricity can be generated by solar power.

At the start of this section I mentioned that vehicle emissions had been targeted because they could be seen as an individual's responsibility. While this is no doubt the case, the matter is by no means wholly in individual hands. For one thing, governments can affect people's attitudes through pricing differentials. Equally, governments can introduce legislation obliging manufacturers to meet certain standards even if consumers are not pressing for those levels to be reached. Moreover, governmental policy affects transport decisions in a more roundabout way. Governments can promote rail transport or favour bicycles; they can develop road systems or discourage the movement of freight by road. And these policy decisions will not only be affected by governments' environmental views. They will also be shaped by more general ideological positions, such as the extent to which they prize individual choice or state intervention. A further influence derives from commercial considerations. Countries whose economies depend on the motor industry will be extremely reluctant to oppose the car. Powerless Third-World governments may equally find that their preferences are overridden by the demands of foreign companies.

Finally, it is worth noting the extent to which the motor industry, composed of immensely powerful firms, is courting the green consumer. They are competing to produce the 'green car' (see the discussion in Chapter 3). And competition is leading them to adopt more and more comprehensive views of what 'green' means: it no longer betokens just fuel economy and low emissions, but also concern for the source, durability and recyclability of component parts.

ENERGY POLICY AND ACID RAIN

A concern with energy has been central to the most all-embracing environmental arguments. Put simply, since the sources of energy which are currently most important (coal, oil and gas) are finite, there is a case for using them as sparingly as possible. Moreover, each of them has other environmental drawbacks: their use contributes to global warming and leads to the production of other pollutants, such as 'acid rain'.

Popular concern about energy grew rapidly after 1973 when the world oil price rose dramatically, in part because of successful organization among the cartel of oil producers (OPEC). Major oil-using countries responded differently to this challenge. The USA, for example, was partially shielded by its own large oil reserves. Many continental European countries sought to increase the efficiency with which they used oil and thus to reduce their imports; they also looked to the natural gas supplies potentially available from the USSR. In addition, France and Belgium opted for the extensive use of nuclear power generation. Norway found that it had major oil and gas reserves under the North Sea and, in any case, its physical geography equipped it for hydroelectric generation. Oil-less Third-World nations, especially those seeking rapid industrialization, faced acute financial difficulties. In some cases, agriculturally derived alcohols could go a small way towards meeting their needs for vehicle fuel but, in the absence of native supplies of fossil fuels, they generally had to borrow money either to buy oil or – as with Taiwan and South Korea for example – to start to go nuclear.

Subsequently, national energy policies have largely been determined by price. The developed world's attempts to loosen its dependence on OPEC helped to keep oil prices relatively low and an approximately steady market was maintained throughout the 1980s. Since energy costs have been manageable, governments have not been impelled to take alternatives as seriously as had seemed likely in the early 1970s. To some extent, environmental campaigners regret the continuing cheapness of oil since they argue that only high prices are likely to motivate attempts to reduce consumption – and therefore pollution and global warming. In the absence of deep anxieties about the affordability of fossil fuels, governments are unlikely to commit large resources to research on energy conservation or on alternative energy sources.

With the rising public interest in green issues, environmentalists see a second opportunity: they can press for changes in energy policy as a way of combating pollution. The single issue which has been of most importance in this regard has been acid rain. Acid rain is produced by the burning of impurities, especially sulphur, contained within fossil fuels. The gases from power stations, boilers and vehicles include sulphur dioxide and oxides of nitrogen. Released into the atmosphere these acidic gases combine with water vapour and turn rainfall into showers of very dilute acid. These acids have been linked to the death of trees, the poisoning of lakes and the corrosion of buildings; sulphur dioxide is also a health hazard. The acidic gases can travel a great distance in the atmosphere before they are brought down in rain; consequently, the countries affected were not always the ones believed to be responsible for causing the pollution. Scandinavian campaigners were already urging recognition of the link between power stations, especially coal-powered ones, and increased acidity in the environment in the early 1970s (Seymour and Girardet 1987, p. 142). Producer countries, particularly those such as the UK and West Germany which at first detected no ecological problems on their own territories, were sceptical. Even if they took the problem seriously, they were much less eager to regard acid rain as the principal cause (see Irwin 1990). The issue became a matter of international controversy and was only resolved in the case of the UK when a European Directive was adopted by environment ministers in November 1988. The development of this controversy, the role of pressure groups and of national and international politics is highly instructive and we shall return to it in greater detail in Chapter 3. At this point it is sufficient to note that there is a confluence of interest in favour of energy efficiency which reduces acid emissions, carbon dixoide production and costs. Energy efficiency receives wide support across the political spectrum; even publications arising from the Conservative Party's 'Bow Group' (Paterson 1989, pp. 99–101) endorse this option strongly.

Finally, within this section it is important to return to nuclear power generation. This issue has long been a subject of public controversy. In essence, its proponents argued that nuclear power would be cheap and plentiful while those opposing it pointed to the dangers associated with nuclear materials. In the UK, the opponents have drawn particular attention to the continuing discharges and periodic leaks (especially at the Sellafield reprocessing plant on the north-west coast of England), to the problems of long-term storage of waste and to the potential dangers from reactors, as evidenced in the explosion at the Chernobyl power station in the USSR in 1986 (see Elsworth 1990, pp. 78–80, 245–6 and 280–93).

The recent rise in the importance of green issues has lent nuclear power a new advantage. The Conservative administration in the UK, which has always favoured nuclear power in order to have a diversity of fuel sources and thus to avoid granting monopoly power to coal workers, has made strong appeals to nuclear power's environmental benefit: it does not lead to global warming. But the nuclear power programme in the UK ran into severe difficulties in 1989. As the *Guardian*'s editorial put it (10 November 1989, p. 22), 'nuclear power was killed not by the greens but by the accountants, discovering an abyss of red in the accounts'.

In the course of the UK government's plans to privatize the electricity supply industry, detailed costings of the component elements were required. Current nuclear power stations have a limited life. Once the costs of cleaning up power station sites at the end of this life and of treating and storing spent fuel were figured into the price of each nuclear power station, nuclear power turned out to be around twice as expensive as non-nuclear. No private company would opt for this so the government had to take the nuclear sector out of the privatization plans. At the same time, for its part the government was unwilling to be left with an expanding and open-ended commitment to fund nuclear power. Accordingly, in November 1989 the UK government reversed its policy of nuclear expansion.

Admittedly, costs are not the only consideration. France, for example, may value the relative independence which its nuclear programme affords. The perceived risks of the technology might decline. But the most rapid growth in power production is likely to be needed in the Third World, where the expense and technical difficulty of nuclear power are likely to be especially problematic. Many environmentalists now argue that a policy of energy efficiency and energy conservation is the best immediate one on a global scale.

Nuclear power is important for one further reason. The response to proposed nuclear installations is the single issue which, more than any other, has prompted environmental protest in the developed world. Opposition to power stations or reprocessing facilities, even when motivated by direct self-interest (for example, people opposing nuclear power near their town or home rather than opposing it as such), has been of great importance in making a connection between environmental issues and practical politics. In environmental activists' terms, it has been responsible for 'politicizing' large numbers of people along green lines (Lowe and Rüdig 1986, pp. 529–33). This issue, the development of green activism, will be considered in Chapters 2 and 3.

CONCLUSION

In this survey, we have reviewed most of the current, pressing environmental issues. Even so, some topics, such as population and general air pollution, have been omitted; it would be impossible to make a definitive listing. Still, just from the issues covered in this chapter we can make two important observations. First, current environmental dangers arise not simply from problems in the natural world but from problems of economic systems, of political choices and of social inequalities. Threats to the world's rain forests are tightly bound to problems of international indebtedness; the hazards faced by elephant populations are tied to national political rivalries. It is important to note that, in nearly every case, environmental dangers pose supernational problems; these need solutions to which national governments are often not well suited. The frequent references to international agreements in this chapter suggest that, at least to a limited extent, governments are beginning to recognize this fact.

The second observation is that, although these environmental threats are largely created by our technological civilization, the problems have commonly been identified through scientific study; sometimes they have been combated scientifically too. Thus, the ozone layer is endangered by chemicals synthesized by Western technologies; yet scientific evidence about the harm caused by CFCs was central to campaigns to protect the ozone layer. Accordingly, green activists may find themselves rather ambivalent about science: they are often critical of it but find they need it too.

These two observations are central to the analyses in the next four chapters. In Chapter 2 we make a start by examining how the leading environmental issues have been placed on the public and political agendas.

NOTES

1 This issue is complicated by the existence of low-level ozone. This gas, as was mentioned in the Introduction, is produced as a result of traffic fumes (and of photocopying). Low-level ozone may be even more effective than stratospheric ozone as an ultra-violet filter. According to a report on BBC Radio 4's 'Science Now' programme (14 November 1989), in some cities ultra-violet radiation at ground level may have decreased between 1968 and 1982 despite the planet's net loss of ozone. For a general introduction to the environmental issues associated with ozone see Gribbin 1988.

2 There are other 'ozone eaters' too. By 1990, UK Friends of the Earth was seeking to stimulate public interest in the threat to the ozone layer from the thinners used in typing correction fluid and from dry-cleaning fluid (tetrachloromethane).

3 Although there has been an *approximate* balance, there have been temperature fluctuations (including the ice ages) which, at least from the human point of view, look pretty extreme. For a possible link between carbon dioxide levels and the extinction of the dinosaurs see the *Guardian* 9 February 1990, p. 23; see also the discussion in Chapter 4.

4 An edited text of her speech was published in the *Guardian* 9 November 1989, p. 7.

5 As mentioned above, the oceans do absorb carbon dioxide and some of the gas is also used by marine plants and by shellfish and related creatures, which build shells of calcium carbonate; see Pearce 1989, pp. 143–51.

6 As with many free market Third-World economies, Brazil experiences a great disparity between rich and poor. While the richest 20 per cent of the population command 67 per cent of the country's household income, the poorest 20 per cent receive a mere 2 per cent. The comparable figures for the USA are 40 per cent and 5 per cent (figures from the *World Development Report* cited in *Time* 6 November 1989, p. 39).

7 The National Trust is very large too but combines nature conservation and heritage preservation; for a useful review of its work see Lowe and Goyder's account, 1983, pp. 138–51.

8 Such arguments are necessarily rather speculative, but important for all that. They do, however, make attractive media copy: see the accounts in *Time* 2 January 1989, pp. 20–3 and in *The Sunday Times Magazine* 26 Febraury 1989, p. 38.

9 Thus, in 1988 a rescue mission was launched on behalf of the giant earwig of St Helena, a monster at eight centimetres in length, which is now threatened by rats. Even an insect keeper from London Zoo admitted that 'It's quite difficult to get people interested in earwigs'; in their support he stressed their 'attractive family life-style. "The females make extremely good mothers"' (*The Independent* 9 February 1988, p. 1).

10 These restrictions have not resulted in complete reassurance since sceptics can argue that, as in any other industry, the rules will occasionally be flouted. It has also been suggested that microscopic traces of the disease-prone tissue will always be left behind when the brain, spinal cord and so on are being cut out. Both kinds of doubt were raised on BBC Radio 4's 'Face the Facts' programme (31 January 1990).

11 It should be borne in mind that radioactive waste need not come from nuclear power stations. According to a report on BBC Radio 4 News on 16 June 1988, the French radioactive waste in question derives from such sources as hospitals.

CHAPTER 2

Putting the green case together

SOCIAL PROBLEMS

As we have seen, the environmental problems described in Chapter 1 are characterized by marked social, political and economic elements. They are not solely about our dealings with the natural world but concern also our dealings with other peoples. There is a strong interaction between these problems and a wide range of social and economic policies. The major responsibility for setting social and economic policies in contemporary societies lies with governments. And, in the West, governments are generally composed of political parties, whether singly or in groups. In their manifestos and in their subsequent actions these party groups take a position on most of the leading issues: they favour the extension or the reduction of income tax; they support the enlargement or diminution of the armed forces; they have particular plans for dealing with unemployment. They even have a view about exactly how far-reaching and pervasive government policies ought to be; right-wing parties, for example, wish to limit the intervention by government and seek to reduce the influence of the 'nanny state'.

But there are many other groups that aim to influence policy. Some of these may be statutory, such as local authorities or committees set up to advise government. Some are pressure groups working for the long-term interest of some segment of society: for example, in the UK, the employers' organization, the Confederation of British Industry (CBI). There are other groups which play a significant role but whose interest is much more narrowly focused, usually on one issue. Typically, these groups address their attention to a particular social problem. Familiar examples from the UK include groups focusing on the homeless at Christmas, groups concerned with the problems of young heroin addicts, and 'Band Aid', the celebrity-backed organization which arose in 1984 in response to famine in Ethiopia.

Such groups have often been successful in bringing an issue to wide public attention and in promoting change in national policy. Accordingly, sociologists have long had an interest in the dynamics of pressure groups and social problems. Of course not all pressure-group organizations deal with a social problem in this sense. Some, as with groups devoted to the needs of the blind, deal with a continuing issue rather than one which is time bound. But it is instructive to start with a time-bound one, such as the response to a famine, to a new illicit drug, or to a newly perceived menace such as football hooliganism. An example which helpfully displays some of the features of social problems is the rise of concern, particularly in the UK, about the portrayal of sex and violence on television. Although there were national guidelines which regulated what could be shown on television, in the late 1960s and 1970s certain groups and individuals began to argue that the regulations were too liberal and that broadcasts contained material harmful to viewers, especially children. Elements from the press as well as some politicians and opinion leaders joined the cause and, before long, a good percentage of the public began to express similar views when interviewed by pollsters. The 'over-explicit' depiction of sex and violence on television had become recognized as a social problem and policy makers were led to change broadcasting standards.

This example of pressure leading to a change in policy is far from being an isolated one and sociologists are understandably intrigued by such occurrences. Early work on social problems suggested, for example, that the problems appeared at times of 'strain' in societal values. On this view, the social problems were not so much important in themselves; rather, they were significant as indices of social turbulence. But work in this mould found it hard to explain what it was that led certain issues to become social problems at any given time. If social problems are only regarded as symptoms it is difficult to understand why turbulence leads to a *particular set* of symptoms.

Subsequent investigations focused instead on the role of the groups which brought the social problem to light. It was then accepted that the interplay needed to be investigated between what were described as the 'objective conditions and the subjective awareness of social problems' (Kitsuse and Spector 1981, p. 199). In other words, the mere fact that there were objective circumstances which constituted a potential problem was not enough for a 'social problem' to emerge. To take what is perhaps the classic example, consider the movement for the abolition of slavery. For at least the two centuries preceding the public prominence of this movement the trade in slaves was integral to the development of European empires. Under laws introduced by the civilized nations of Europe, human beings were daily handled as commodities and treated more severely than domestic animals. The objective conditions behind the social problem of slavery were certainly present. Yet slavery was not perceived as a social problem at all. The task of the abolitionists was to lead opinion formers and the public to see the matter in a different light.

In the sociological study of social problems a controversy has arisen. No one would now argue that the objective conditions in themselves (say, the existence of slavery or the depiction of much explicit violence on television) are enough to promote awareness of a social problem. The subject of dispute is whether the actual existence of the objective conditions is necessary before a social problem can arise. At first sight this might seem a peculiar notion. Surely, it might be said, the abolitionists could only make their case if slavery existed and if some slaves, at least, were badly treated. But the case of 'over-explicit' television broadcasts helpfully points in the other direction. While people would no doubt agree that both sex and violence are shown on television, it would be much harder to establish as a 'fact' that there is *too much*. The 'too much' claim appears to be more of a judgement than a factual report.

Kitsuse and Spector have taken the lead in arguing that sociologists concerned with social problems should suspend any interest in whether the objective circumstances merit the existence of a social problem or not (Spector and Kitsuse 1977). (It is not that social scientists do not care about such questions; they simply realize that their own views on them do not explain why the public comes to adopt a given opinion.) Instead, they should focus on the social processes involved in bringing an issue to public attention as a social problem. For Kitsuse and Spector (1981, p. 201),

> The existence of social problems depends on the continued existence of groups or agencies that define some condition as a problem and attempt to do something about it. To ask what are the effective causes of social problems, or what keeps social problems activities going, is to ask what keeps these various groups going.

On this view, the sociologist should not explain the existence of public anxieties about 'over-explicit' television by referring to the immorality of the sex and violence depicted on television. (Indeed, why entrust sociologists with such moral judgements?) Rather, the anxieties are explicable in the light of the promotional activities of campaigning groups.

Two consequences follow from this approach. First, it becomes important to inquire into the mechanisms by which a social problem comes to public attention in the first place. If the problem is not simply a reflection of problematic objective conditions, how did it come to the fore? Second, one needs to discover what it is that accounts for continued interest in a particular social problem. Again in Kitsuse and Spector's words, 'The central problem for a theory of social problems ... is to account for the *emergence* and *maintenance* of claim-making and responding activities' (1981, p. 201, emphasis added).

The first question, about the origin of social problems, is generally answered in terms of moral entrepreneurship (see Becker 1973, pp. 147–55). Certain persons develop a concern with some aspect of society which they regard as problematic; they then commit their energies to raising the public visibility of this 'problem'. Characteristically, they seek to enlist the interest of the press and the media, they lobby politicians, community leaders and, often, religious authorities, and they set about forming organizations to forward their cause and to persuade other people of its merits. The term 'entrepreneur' captures very successfully the kinds of activities in which they have to engage:

they must find a market for their ideas and compete with other campaigning groups for resources such as press coverage and public attention.

Having brought about the initial recognition of a social problem, the entrepreneur's or the group's work is not finished. They face a second challenge in keeping the problem in the public eye and in exerting the pressure needed to bring about changes in attitudes, policy, or legislation. Those concerned with a social problem seldom find themselves in a position where their claims are fully met. Either they may be offered a compromise or they may perceive new dimensions to the original problem. At the same time, groups involved in trying to remedy a social problem find that there are many demands on them: there are the demands of their supporters or membership, there is the need to manage relationships with other pressure groups and with official agencies and there are nearly always financial difficulties. In all, groups seldom fade away because their demands have been met. On the contrary, it is common for groups either to collapse under the weight of demands on them or to become so established, or routinized, that even if their original goal is satisfied they develop new aims. In the process of developing these new aims they generally need to extend their original social problem claim.

Finally in this section, it is important to return to the question of the reality of the supposed social problem. Kitsuse and Spector again provide a good starting point here. They note that like-minded authors have commonly supposed that 'group definitions of social problems *usually do* have reference to some empirically verifiable social conditions' (1981, p. 200, original emphasis). Whole groups of people do not usually get 'upset over "nothing"'. Still, their own position is that

> one need not assume nor explain the existence of this objective condition; indeed, to do so would deflect attention from investigation of the definitional process. The definition *may* be accompanied by empirically verifiable claims about the scale, intensity, distribution, and effects of the imputed social conditions: but it *may not* and theoretically it *need not*. (1981, pp. 200–1, original emphases)

People may be genuinely upset by the prospect of an invasion by wholly fictitious aliens; at the same time, they may remain unperturbed by the threats implied in the worldwide stockpiling of chemical and biological weapons.[1] The question of the reality of environmental problems will arise later in this chapter and be examined in more detail in Chapter 4.

ENVIRONMENTAL PROBLEMS AS SOCIAL PROBLEMS

Readers will not be surprised to learn that the purpose of this chapter is to consider the environmental issues outlined in Chapter 1 in the light of the social problems perspective, and to analyse the green movement as a collection of agencies making 'social problem claims'. This is not done for the sake of bolstering a sociological theory but because this perspective allows us to appreciate how the green movement has come to assume the shape it has at the beginning of the 1990s. A book written even a few years ago (for example the excellent Pye-Smith and Rose 1984) would have presented pressure groups struggling to create public concern about a social problem. Straightforwardly campaigning books would have exhorted their readers to take the issues seriously (Porritt 1984). Now, with green issues high on the political and public agendas, it might be tempting to argue simply that the objective problem has finally forced itself into the public consciousness. The social problems perspective prevents us from falling into that way of rewriting history; it leads us to ask how it is that environmental issues have come to be seen as an objective social problem. It also encourages us to examine processes internal to the green movement. There are, as we have seen, many strands to the movement. This perspective leads us to inquire how certain problems have come to the fore within the overall green case, how others have suffered relative neglect and why some organizations have prospered. It also indicates some of the things which can be anticipated from the green movement.

As was illustrated in the Introduction, green issues are now brought before the public by politicians, the media and even by advertising agencies. But this high level of general enthusiasm is a recent development. Previously the most significant actors were organizations which lobbied, campaigned and took part in publicity campaigns on behalf of the environment. For the UK, the most significant review of environmental organizations has been undertaken by Lowe and Goyder (1983). During 1979–80 they conducted a survey of seventy-seven national voluntary organizations concerned with the environment. In each case, these authors inquired into the group's aims. They also examined such characteristics as the membership, the income, the staffing and the internal decision-making structure of the groups. Additionally, they sought the groups' views on matters such as the responsiveness of government departments. On the basis of the groups' reports about the other organizations with which they were in regular communication, Lowe and Goyder (1983, p. 81) were able to classify them according to four main emphases: conservation (for example, the Fauna and Flora Preservation Society), recreation (the Ramblers' Association), amenity (the Building Conservation Trust), and resources (covering issues such as transport and pollution).

Within each of these areas there exists a variety of organizations, differentiated in various ways. For example, some are chiefly professional organizations while others have a predominantly lay membership (one can contrast the British Trust for Ornithology with the Royal Society for the Protection of Birds, see below). Some have a long and venerable history while others are of recent formation (the RSPB is now over a century old; Greenpeace has barely reached the age of 20). Some are marked by very specific goals while others have a more general orientation (bat preservation groups can be contrasted with Greenpeace's wide campaigning style). Lowe and Goyder suggest that it is hard to generalize about the characteristics of a successful organization. Apart from the finding that resources are generally a limiting factor so that, by and large, a big membership is beneficial, regular tendencies are hard to spot. This is due to the complexity of the environmental phenomena with which the groups are dealing and to the rapidly changing context of green politics. Thus, rather than seek to generalize at this stage I will present a short series of profiles of groups. These will allow patterns in the history, structure, and evolution of aims to be observed. At the same time it will allow some updating of the information supplied by Lowe and Goyder. To begin with I will turn to one organization discussed at some length also by Lowe and Goyder (1983, pp. 152–62), the Royal Society for Nature Conservation (RSNC). The other two profiled groups are not reviewed by these authors in depth.

THE ROYAL SOCIETY FOR NATURE CONSERVATION

Early in the twentieth century the threat to certain highly prized British wildlife sites was already beginning to be acknowledged. A leading patron of natural history, Charles Rothschild, responded in 1912 by founding a Society for the Promotion of Nature Reserves (SPNR). At the outset the society's aim was not to run reserves itself but to encourage others, particularly the National Trust, to acquire them. Since its task was primarily promotional, the society was able to be small and self-consciously to comprise only the élite. Indeed, entire control was constitutionally accorded to the fifty members of its council; it was intended that they should use their influence with landowners and other potential patrons to endow natural history.

Yet, as Lowe and Goyder make clear, considering the prominence of some of its members, the organization achieved surprisingly little up until the Second World War. In part this was due to the formal features of the organization. The members of the ruling council were elected for life so that the early cohort of leaders tended to age together. The society could not easily expand its membership since people who wished to join could only become associate members, with no say in the running of the group. For its own part, the society was not empowered to charge associate members a fee so it had little incentive to welcome them. Associate members were actually a financial liability to the organization. For these reasons, the SPNR was unable to take advantage of the growth in popular interest in the countryside, hiking and cycling which supplied the membership for groups such as the Ramblers' Association (Stevenson 1984, pp. 236–41 and 392–3). In any case, farming was generally depressed and very far from intensive. The countryside was not systematically imperilled and, outside of some very special contexts, there seemed little need for nature reserves.

Wartime brought great changes to the fortunes of the society. Its recommendation that there should be a national review of wildlife and of the need for nature reserves was adopted by the government and turned into a proposal for postwar action, a plan 'which now commended itself for its obvious symbolic value in helping to sustain morale during a period of intense national sacrifice' (Lowe and Goyder 1983, p. 154). As part of official preparations for postwar reconstruction a committee to look into nature reserves was set up through the SPNR. The society thus acquired official responsibilities and a new status. The investigation of the need for nature reserves achieved important work and, as Nicholson (1972, p. 183) drolly notes,

> It is an ironic commentary on the workings of the British system of government that it should have been possible under heavy German bombing, and subject to petrol rationing, blackout and absence on military service of so many able-bodied observers, at last to carry through, within a mere couple of years, a survey and review, which had clearly been urgently needed since the previous century. This was thanks to the wartime suspension of working of the normal British mechanisms for ensuring inaction.

Under the peculiar circumstances of wartime the small, élite composition of the SPNR was, ironically, an advantage. Moreover, the fact that it was not supported by a wide public membership and lacked the ethos of a combative pressure group meant that it had few established enemies and suffered from little internal dissension.

After the war, the government established an official body, the Nature Conservancy, concerned with acquiring and managing nature reserves and with promoting ecological research. Owing to its role in the setting up of this body, the SPNR once again commanded considerable influence; there was, for example, extensive overlap between the councils of the Nature Conservancy and of the SPNR (Lowe and Goyder 1983, p. 155). Initially it appeared that the Nature Conservancy, 'the first official science-based environmental conservation agency in the world' (Nicholson 1987, p. 95), would take over the role of the voluntary body and make it redundant. However, as Nicholson (who assumed the general-directorship in 1952) states (1987, p. 99):

> far from superseding the voluntary movement, as had wrongly been assumed by some of its earlier leaders, the Nature Conservancy under my direction had opened up new fields of opportunity that enabled the enrolled membership to expand on a scale hitherto undreamt of, and in so doing to promote and sustain an increased role and support for the Conservancy itself.

This enhanced role operated in two ways. First, as Nicholson (1987, p. 98) points out, there was a set of mutual interests between the official body and groups, particularly local and even short-lived ones, objecting to some environmental problem such as the loss of a wildlife site. These latter groups 'could benefit by the Conservancy's official status, contacts and information, while it could gain no less advantage from their ability overtly to campaign against misbehaving official bodies, and to whip up political and other support'. This potential alliance was strengthened by occasional grant aiding and by an 'unconventional kind of official initiative' by which Nicholson 'promoted the creation of a federation' to link the work of voluntary bodies, the Council for Nature. At its launch in 1958 it was headed by Lord Hurcomb, president of the SPNR and a leading officer of the Nature Conservancy.

The second path turned out to be the basis for the SPNR's future development. Before the foundation of the Nature Conservancy there already existed a local naturalists' group in each of Yorkshire, Norfolk and Lincolnshire. They had formed the kernel of the SPNR-inspired survey work in their areas. Even after the Nature Conservancy had come into being, members of these groups believed that they should retain a role in monitoring reserves and sites in their areas; after all, they had local knowledge, expertise and enthusiasm. Once again Nicholson, allied with Hurcomb, played a large role in shaping developments; these two men persuaded the SPNR to welcome advocates of these groups (now referred to as wildlife trusts but then known as the county trusts) on to its council. Once inside the society, the trusts' representative worked on a programme of reform. The trusts and the SPNR entered into a mutually profitable arrangement whereby the society became the co-ordinating body for the trusts. To this exchange the society contributed its name and reputation, its contacts and its financial resources. For their part the trusts brought members, some reserves and the sense of mission which the SPNR then lacked (Lowe and Goyder 1983, p. 156).

The SPNR was not the sole beneficiary of this deal. The Nature Conservancy also profited from the willingness of local volunteers to supplement its programme of conservation work. In particular, the county trusts – which grew very rapidly in number in the early 1960s – contributed to the Conservancy's work in the following ways. They helped with maintenance work on the declared wildlife sites, the Sites of Special Scientific Interest (SSSIs), which were too numerous for the Conservancy's staff to manage. They assisted in surveying these sites and in drawing up management agreements with the owners. Equally, the county trusts undertook their own fund-raising work and began to acquire more nature reserves. Their preferred sites tended to be those whose conservation and scientific value had been recognized, in short, SSSIs. Their practice thus dovetailed very closely with the official agency's conservation priorities. In addition, they were well placed to engage in school visits and other educational work, in the provision of information and of visitors' centres at reserves, and in the supplying of advice to landowners, local authorities and other bodies (Lowe and Goyder 1983, p. 158). In return the Nature Conservancy provided grant aid to the SPNR and the county trusts.

Essentially the same arrangement has endured since the 1960s. The SPNR recognized that its aim was no longer purely to encourage nature reserves and accordingly incorporated 'nature conservation' into its title in 1977, becoming the SPNC. In 1981 the name changed again since it was permitted to describe itself as the Royal Society for Nature Conservation; it now enjoys the patronage of the Prince of Wales. Its growth has continued; by the end of 1989 there were forty-eight wildlife trusts and an official membership of around 204,000 (RSNC 1989a, p. i).[2] The majority of wildlife trusts enjoy the support of paid staff and their work in reserve acquisition and management, and in education and promotion continues.

There are sources of tension however. One concerns disparities between the trusts themselves. Some are large, well endowed and active. The Norfolk Trust, for example, runs extensive and popular holiday programmes and other money-making ventures. The Avon Trust operates an environmental consultancy. The possibility of carrying out 'environmental audits' for local companies which are seeking to promote their green credentials is a related service which, as will be seen in the next chapter, is proving attractive to some wildlife trusts. Finally, the group in Northern Ireland (the Ulster Wildlife Trust) although not among the leaders in terms of membership, is active and locally influential; in part this arises because it benefits from unusually generous governmental financial aid due, in large measure, to the region's depressed economy. In contrast, many other trusts are small, have little local influence and struggle to maintain a cadre of salaried staff. Commonly these differences are self-reinforcing; big trusts have the resources to generate even more income, publicity and membership. The RSNC, as their confederation, faces difficulties in meeting all their needs simultaneously.

A degree of tension also characterizes the relationship between the RSNC and the trusts. The RSNC provides central services to the wildlife trusts, including the publication of the magazine *Natural World* and the mounting of training courses. But there is a constant potential for conflict over the question, is the central body just a servant to the trusts' joint needs or should it adopt a leading role? In part, this is simply a contest for control. Is the RSNC a distinctive organization or is it only the 'society for co-ordinating wildlife trusts'? Also in part, the contest has become a problem for publicity and marketing. While Greenpeace, Friends of the Earth, the RSPB and other national groups can organize national recruiting campaigns this is harder for a federation of wildlife trusts, part of whose appeal is precisely their regional character. Thirdly, it has also become a question of ideology. By their nature, the trusts are based on wildlife conservation in specific localities. Pye-Smith and Rose's judgement (1984, p. 187) is now too harsh but is still telling: 'Trusts vary greatly but are almost all dominated by the "county set" (or at least people who aspire to it!). The trusts are good at raising money to acquire small Nature Reserves.'

For their part, staff of the RSNC are more inclined to compare their organization with those adopting the most pioneering positions in the green movement. Freed from affiliation to a specific county or region, they are very aware of the internationalization and politicization of the green movement. In 1988, for example, the RSNC conference for trusts' conservation staff featured a stirring presentation by Lord Melchett of Greenpeace, stressing the successes achieved through direct action. In the same year, the gathering of education officers was encouraged to examine global issues linking ecological problems with development. These would be new and unfamiliar waters for many of the wildlife trusts.

Finally, the relationship between the Nature Conservancy (since 1973, the Nature Conservancy Council (NCC)) and the RSNC together with its trusts, while close, has not always been entirely harmonious. When harmony has been absent it has usually been because the society considers that the NCC should be more vigorous. In its publication *Losing Ground* (RSNC 1989b, pp. 14–15) the RSNC states that the NCC is

> suffering from lack of resources and [does] not have the manpower to identify all the sites meeting the criteria for designation [as SSSIs], nor to initiate the notification procedure. Lack of staff is forcing the NCC to ignore wildlife sites that are not under imminent threat. Perhaps it considers there to be little point in notifying new sites if the resources to protect properly those which have been designated are lacking?

The RSNC proposes that all intended SSSIs should be notified within five years. In response to this perceived threat to valuable sites some members of wildlife trusts have argued that SSSIs should be acquired by trusts, since only then would wildlife be safeguarded from changes in government policy and be given real protection – protection which SSSI designation fails to provide.

The situation was made even more complex at the end of 1989 when the UK government announced its plans to devolve the Scottish and the Welsh parts of the NCC and to combine them with the respective Countryside Commissions (the official amenity agencies) (*Guardian* 10 November 1989, p. 25). The RSNC opposes this move, fearing that the scientific basis of national conservation would be dispersed and that, for example, forestry interests in Scotland would have more influence over a local body than over the NCC. If, as seems likely, the split goes ahead tensions between the RSNC and the elements of the restyled NCC are likely to increase.

To conclude this section, a number of observations can be made. The first point is that the RSNC's concern with nature conservation has been firmly based on a scientific interest. From the outset it was an élite and scientific organization. Its chief concern in practising conservation was to preserve areas of *scientific* interest, an emphasis later enshrined in the law and practice of the official body, the NCC. The RSNC's and the trusts' scientific credentials have been important in their relationship with government, in establishing themselves as local sources of authoritative advice, and in new departures such as environmental consultancies.

External factors have shaped its development also. As Lowe and Goyder observe, 'The success of its war-time lobbying demonstrates how dependent the fortunes of a pressure group can be on changes in the political context quite beyond its control' (1983, p. 162). More recently, the wildlife trusts have been strongly affected by the availability of labour provided through the government's job creation schemes, particularly the Community Programme. However, as the levels of recorded unemployment fell in the late 1980s these schemes were reduced, leaving some trusts understaffed. The RSNC has also had to compete with other environmental pressure groups which threaten to focus on its favoured issues. Thus, in 1990 both the RSNC and Friends of the Earth (FOE) launched peatland campaigns, although in this instance there was a large measure of co-operation. The RSNC cannot afford to allow groups such as FOE and Greenpeace to capture the highest profile issues and to attract away its supporters and sponsors.

The social problems perspective allows us to take an overall view of the development of the RSNC. Although its growth has been shaped by political and historical circumstances far beyond its own control, the following central point can be made. In its long and venerable history the RSNC has shaped what nature conservation means. Owing largely to the work of this organization, nature conservation focuses on scientific criteria (rather than, say, amenity or aesthetic ones) and wildlife sites are assessed as Sites of Special *Scientific* Interest. Thus the RSNC has moulded official conservation practice in the UK. The RSNC has made the threat to endangered sites into a social problem; at the same time it has led many in the conservation 'establishment' to equate environmental problems with threats to wildlife and nature conservation.

THE ROYAL SOCIETY FOR THE
PROTECTION OF BIRDS

In 1989 the Royal Society for the Protection of Birds celebrated its centenary. The RSPB styles itself the biggest, single-issue conservation group in Europe and boasts over half a million members on top of the 100,000 young people enrolled as 'young ornithologists' (Samstag 1988, p. 149).[3] Its history is a curious amalgam of continuity and change. In terms of continuity, the society has been steadfast in its focus on birds and their needs. Unlike the RSNC which has changed its function several times, and unlike Greenpeace, which, as will be seen, has regularly switched its target, the RSPB has retained one clear, principal commitment. However, the interpretation of that commitment has altered considerably.

The RSPB is proud of its rather curious origin. It emerged from the combination of two groups (one in Manchester, one in Croydon, just south of London) which were formed to oppose the use of feathers in the fashion trade, particularly by milliners. The trade consumed tons of feathers annually; on average six birds were killed to supply every ounce. The campaigners insisted that this represented a vast, wasteful and heedless slaughter, one which would not be tolerated in the case of other kinds of animals. After all, the slaughtered birds' bodies were not even used for meat. (Readers will recognize the similarity to current arguments about the fur trade.)

The originating groups had been largely composed of women; their targets were women too. An attempt was made to persuade women to take a pledge not to wear feathers except those from the ostrich (from which they can apparently be taken when the bird is alive). This campaign was organized in a decentralized way. The formation of local groups all over the country was encouraged. In turn, these groups would enrol ordinary members for a subscription of two pence.

Female dominance did not last long, however, and in 1892 W. H. Hudson, the ornithologist, assumed the role of chairman despite his celebrated lack of administrative skills. Three years later he passed the mantle to another man, this time an able leader. Recruitment was brisk and by 1898 the society could claim 152 branches and 20,000 ordinary members (Sheail 1976, p. 13). Still, as Samstag points out (1988, p. 26),

> Throughout this early, heady period of expansion, and for many decades afterwards, the Society was to maintain its character – verging, indeed, on caricature – as the archetypal British voluntary organization operating from a position of hereditary privilege, run mainly by and for women.

As this quotation implies, from an early stage the society enjoyed the support of élite figures. There was even support from royalty, some of it of a practical kind. Thus, by royal command, especially rare plumes were withdrawn from military dress in 1899 and in 1906 Queen Alexandra offered the society a letter for publication in which she endorsed the general campaign against the fashion trade's use of plumage (Samstag 1988, p. 40). Pressure for legislative change was building up but parliamentary action was delayed by the the First World War. However, although membership was by then in decline, an Act was passed in 1921 prohibiting the import of plumage. To all intents and purposes the trade ceased the following year (see Lowe 1983, p. 333).

During these first three decades the society's central argument had been that huge numbers of birds around the whole globe were dying for a trivial end. Whole species were threatened merely for the sake of passing fashion. According to Ian Prestt, the RSPB's Director-General, this style of argument was retained into the next phase in the society's development, a period in which the main concern was with wild bird protection within the

UK.[4] Several species, particularly birds of prey, were threatened by the actions of individuals, for example by egg collectors, by those seeking stuffed trophies and by gamekeepers. This was not the sole threat; there was anxiety about oil spillages and about agricultural chemicals even in the 1920s (Samstag 1988, p. 41). There were also more obscure threats, such as the regular finding that many migrating birds met their deaths around lighthouses. It was believed that the birds were attracted to lighthouses by night, that they circled the lights and finally fell exhausted into the sea in vast numbers. Accordingly, perches were placed around selected lights (Sheail 1976, p. 15). More significantly for the long-term development of the society, there was also growing interest in bird watching. Watchers were drawn to the society because it began to hold leases on some important breeding grounds (Hammond 1983, p. 159).

But, as Prestt observed, these causes were much less popular than the opposition to the plumage trade and by 1939 the membership was below 5,000. In wartime it fell still further. Hammond (1983, p. 160) cites additional reasons for this decline. By the mid-1930s the core of the ruling council – as had been the case with the SPNR – was ageing and becoming set in its ways. Criticism was voiced of the leadership it offered; it was held to be administratively costly, rigid, and slow to take the initiative over new issues such as the treatment of caged birds. In an uncommonly lively AGM in 1936 it was decided that a committee should be established to look into the running of the society. The reforms it proposed were largely adopted and, although handicapped by the war, the organization was placed to recover quickly once peace arrived. As Sheail observes (1976, p. 14), the RSPB 'expanded from being simply an anti-plumage movement into an organization working for the protection of wild birds in every way and by all available means'. While this shift in emphasis may be detected, as Sheail maintains, from early this century, it was only after 1945 that the society began to seize the opportunities presented by this wide brief.

After the war bird watching grew as a pastime, as did specialist knowledge of bird behaviour and of habitat management (Hammond 1983, p. 161). Such specialist skills were promoted by the British Trust for Ornithology, a group for advancing scientific knowledge of birds founded in 1933 by, among others, Max Nicholson (Nicholson 1987, p. 90). The RSPB grew along with these trends, consciously adopting a more popular image; according to Prestt, it even sought advice from the Reader's Digest Association on how to popularize itself. Among its concerns there were some projects with high news value. For example, birds were recovered from the frequent oil spills which troubled the British coast, especially in the wake of the infamous Torrey Canyon wreck on the Isles of Scilly in 1967 (Nicholson 1987, p. 46). Perhaps even more newsworthy was the return of birds thought lost to Britain. The osprey returned to breed in 1959 (Samstag 1988, p. 83). The preceding year it had also returned and laid eggs but, despite the presence of an RSPB guard, the eggs had been stolen. In 1959 the RSPB watchers again mounted a guard on the breeding site and this time sawed away the lower branches of the tree so that ascent to the nest was virtually impossible. As soon as the eggs hatched the RSPB made the story public. This caused some disquiet within the society since it was feared that publicity would draw onlookers who might disturb the birds. But the publicity value far outweighed this danger. Subsequently the RSPB was involved in the scheme to reintroduce the white-tailed sea eagle (1988, p. 153), which again provided many 'photo-opportunities'. A third activity with a high public profile was the pursuit and prosecution of bird and egg collectors. In each case the RSPB showed that it had learned how to maximize the story's appeal to the mass media. In particular, they successfully capitalized on the photogenic quality of many birds.

If in 1959 there was a fear that birds would be endangered by the numbers of visitors, the threat has increased greatly since then with the growth of the hobby and the advent of the fanatical bird watchers, known collectively as 'twitchers'. The stereotypical twitcher is determined to see every rarity brought to the UK by freak weather or sheer chance. Information about rarities, once supplied through an informal grape-vine, would lead to the poor bird being surrounded by a pack of observers. Such unseemly devotion was something of an embarrassment to the RSPB, although the genuine commitment of the twitchers could hardly be doubted. The society now seeks to regulate their behaviour by providing a telephone 'hotline' with authoritative information (see *Guardian* 2 March 1990, p. 23) and by encouraging more disciplined behaviour at the sites. Although far from typical members of the RSPB, the twitchers reflect two of its most important characteristics. In their knowledge of birds they mirror the depth of natural history expertise possessed by the society. Equally, in their almost fanatical single-mindedness they display the RSPB's exclusive commitment to birds.

Indeed, as was made clear in Simon Jenkins's Radio 4 documentary on the RSPB (see note 3), the society is bound to the interests of birds even if this conflicts with some members' personal interests. For example, in the negotiations conducted during 1989 over the proposed rail route from London, through Kent, to the Channel Tunnel, the RSPB campaigned for estuaries to be left undisturbed even though this was probably contrary to the wishes of some Kentish members who wanted the railway to be kept well away from their villages.

The question of expertise is important in regard to the internal politics of the society. Although the original tendency towards élitism might be thought to persist – the RSPB is still well patronized by 'the great and the good' – it is moderated by increasing meritocracy. Quite simply, detailed knowledge about birds counts for a great deal. Formal rules have also been changed; unlike the early situation, members of the ruling council now have only a five-year term and they are elected by the membership. However, according to Simon Jenkins's account, vacancies are still usually filled by candidates proposed by the existing council. But the increasing number of salaried staff means that a greater share of management is now taken by those appointed for their knowledge of birds, conservation, planning law and so on.

An increasingly important part of the society's activity is the acquisition of reserves. This conservation strategy had been tried as early as the 1920s but the society was sometimes confounded by the behaviour of neighbouring landowners (Sheail, 1976, p. 176). Its acquisitions policy was also attacked as rather unsystematic (Hammond 1983, p. 159). Still, areas important for the presence of a particularly rare bird were acquired and management experience grew. By the 1980s, according to Samstag (1988, p. 70), the RSPB was 'unstinting in its pursuit of land'. This enthusiasm for reserves reflects a point made in Chapter

1, that the society now aims to conserve bird habitats rather than birds *per se*. Instead of directing attention at individual birds (except when they represent a high proportion of the UK population), the society attends to conserving characteristic habitats where birds can feed, breed or over-winter.[5] The current tally of reserves is 118. Through this focus on habitat the society has been led to conserve species other than birds, for example trees off which they feed or animals which they consume. In this way the society's conservational interests have become broader.

This broadening of perspective can take a geographical dimension too. In recent years the argument has increasingly been made that there is little point in conserving migratory birds' habitats in the UK if the sites they use elsewhere are endangered. The society may well be wasting money on expensive conservation exercises only to find that the birds are shot over the Mediterranean or have had their winter feeding grounds destroyed. Consequently the RSPB has expanded internationally, providing training and support for organizations around the globe. It even, in the case of rare roseate terns which were not protected once they had migrated to West Africa, collaborated with the Ghanaian government (Samstag, 1988, p. 71). From this position, it is a short step to concern about birds which have no connection with the UK. And since many of the most exotic of the world's birds inhabit the rain forests, this provided the RSPB with its own, distinctive reason for joining in one of the most high-profile conservation issues of the late 1980s.

The final point arising from the concern with reserves is that land acquisition is obviously costly. To meet these demands the RSPB has developed considerable commercial acumen. It uses a wide range of business techniques in targeting donors and sponsors. It even offers its own 'Visa' credit card (the RSNC has recently followed suit with a 'Mastercard'). According to Simon Jenkins, the RSPB has an enviable reputation for encouraging generosity amongst its members and a record of fund-raising successes. Certainly, its annual income now runs to millions of pounds and this affords a large degree of independence from government.

The case of the RSPB shows the organization very clearly as a 'social problem claims making' body. Initially, these claims concerned the plumage trade, later the UK's wild birds and, later still, bird habitats considered internationally. By its single-minded focus on birds' needs and by its avoidance of damaging internal wrangles over wildfowl shooting (the discussion of which is constitutionally outlawed), the society has succeeded in generating wide attention and sympathy for the problems of birds. The attractiveness of birds, and their suitability as subjects for photography and television, have contributed to the RSPB's successful advocacy of their case. But, as with the RSNC, its success has acted to shape what nature conservation means in practical terms. While birds may get a good deal in the UK, it is not clear that fish or even plants do so well. It might even be argued that birds' needs have been placed above the demands of certain human interest groups; in some respects they are probably more ably represented than certain minority groups. In other words, by placing birds at the centre of nature conservation activity, the RSPB has had the effect of contributing to the marginalization of other issues.

GREENPEACE

Greenpeace is celebrated for its imaginative and daring campaigning through direct action. Compared to the RSNC and RSPB it has only a short history. Officially it dates from a Canadian anti-nuclear venture begun in 1971, although plans for the protest had been put forward as early as 1969. An authorized history has recently been published (Brown and May 1989) and much of the following draws on this account. The organization's first objective was to protest against US nuclear testing in the Aleutian Islands, which lie to the west of Alaska. The idea was to sail a boat, renamed the *Greenpeace*, close to the test site but just outside US jurisdiction. The presence of the boat, and of the vulnerable crew, was intended to prevent the American armed forces from detonating the explosion. Although the boat was crewed by US citizens as well as Canadians, the fact that the vessel itself and the base from which it operated were Canadian was useful in securing a degree of freedom from US legal authority. All the same, the US government still had control over timing and they used this weapon to the full

They delayed the nuclear explosion once the boat neared the test site and waited for the crew's food, money and patience to become exhausted. Since this was Greenpeace's first venture, their resources were meagre and after less than a month they turned back towards Vancouver.

Even as they returned, a second boat – chartered out of money raised largely because of publicity from the *Greenpeace* – was sailing towards the test site. But before it was close enough to inhibit the military, the bomb was detonated. Although the campaigners therefore failed to achieve their first objective, the prevention of this particular nuclear test, they were not disheartened for, a few months later, at the start of 1972, the US government announced the cessation of testing in the Aleutians.

Fuelled by this reversal of government policy and by the support and media attention it had attracted in Canada, Greenpeace turned its attention to a key anti-nuclear target: the French testing of nuclear weapons in the atmosphere above Moruroa Atoll in the South Pacific Ocean. A small crew on a twelve-metre boat accordingly departed from Auckland, again aiming to enter the test area and to embarrass the military authorities. Like the Americans, the French tried to use their control over timing to discourage the protestors. Additionally, they sent large, intimidating boats very close to 'monitor' the yacht. They sought to scare the crew away by issuing warnings about the impending explosion. But the crew withstood the dangers and, thanks to a constant flow of press releases, something of the drama of the story was relayed in major European newspapers. Finally, the protest was called off after a collision between the yacht and a French minesweeper (for a compelling recollection of these events see McTaggart 1978, pp. 171–88).

The following summer, 1973, saw a repeat of the protest except on this occasion French military personnel boarded the Greenpeace yacht at an early stage, and in the ensuing struggle, the boat's captain, a Canadian was badly injured. Conflicting accounts of the fight were provided but the Canadian press, persuaded by photographs smuggled back by the crew, championed their national's case, claiming that he had been assaulted. (For his own account of the beatings he received, see McTaggart 1978, pp. 279–91). Encouraged by this popular interest the captain,

David McTaggart, travelled to Paris in 1974 to take the French authorities to court. One year later he received damages for the ramming of his boat. But in the following year his second claim, that his boat had been boarded illegally, was rejected; the boarding was deemed to have been a matter of state security. Still, the French testing policy was altered in 1974, a change which Greenpeace was happy to attribute to its campaigning.

Up until the mid-1970s Greenpeace was exclusively anti-nuclear in deed if not in ideology. Yet from the outset the boats had been decorated with pro-ecology as well as anti-nuclear symbols. And the protest in the Aleutian Islands had been justified by a concern for the native wildlife. But the first overtly non-nuclear campaign was opposed by some in the movement. Thus far the group had gained considerable publicity, created a strong sense of identity and seen the fulfilment of some of its policy objectives. But it hardly had an administrative centre or a fund-raising strategy. These began to develop around a new project, initiated in 1975. Its focus was on whaling. Greenpeace's aim was to locate whaling fleets in the Pacific, to try to persuade the crews of the cruelty of their actions, and to disrupt the whale hunt. To accomplish these tasks the campaigners took with them inflatable dinghies with powerful motors, the kind the French military had earlier used to board their protest yacht. They also took musical instruments with which to serenade the whales and, most important, film cameras to document their work. It was on this protest that they pioneered the method of placing volunteers in dinghies between the whales and the harpoons. Although the earlier volunteers had faced considerable danger by entering nuclear test zones, photographs showing Greenpeace volunteers in the sights of harpoon guns made the personal risks strikingly apparent.

The impact of direct action could hardly be doubted, particularly its publicity and media value. These were gripping, well-documented stories displaying great daring. From 1976 the same general approach was adopted towards seal culling; here again the protestors placed themselves between the seals and the huntsmen. The organization had entered an improving spiral. The activities fed the media's interest; the press coverage encouraged people to contribute to the campaigns or to become members. Greenpeace groups flourished during this period, particularly in Europe: national organizations were formed in France (1977), the UK (1977) and The Netherlands (1978).

The UK was also the source of the *Rainbow Warrior*, a ship purchased for an anti-whaling campaign off Iceland in 1978. In the next two years the vessel was used for anti-whaling work, but also for a protest against seal culling in Scotland and for action against the marine dumping of drums of radioactive waste. In the latter case, the volunteers again adapted their earlier protest techniques, this time seeking to place their dinghies alongside the ships at the point at which the drums were dropped into the sea.

All the time that Greenpeace was running a small number of protests and allowing each to raise its own funds, its devolved structure was satisfactory. But it was increasingly difficult to hold together an international organization encompassing groups with different priorities. There was also a need to raise money in a disciplined way. These tensions became manifest in a conflict between the Canadian and US groups. South of the border there were increasingly many active groups, a number of them well able to raise funds. The Vancouver office was in serious debt yet, according to Brown and May (1989, p. 65), US groups

> were increasingly successful at raising funds, and Vancouver felt they were taking advantage of the Greenpeace name – the name that Vancouver had done so much to build up. The climax came when Greenpeace Vancouver sued the office in San Francisco for violation of trademark agreements. San Francisco retaliated by suing for slander.

A compromise was reached under the influence of McTaggart, who was now based in Europe but retained influence in Canada. Greenpeace Europe cleared the debts once all the branches agreed to come under the co-ordinating umbrella of a new body, Greenpeace International (see Eyerman and Jamison 1989, pp. 103–9). The international body was financed out of local revenues and was composed of representatives from Europe, North America and Australasia. Local groups were free to devise their own campaigns but the confederated structure was intended to preclude future competition.

Diversification continued with campaigns against dolphin slaughters in Japan, against the marine dumping of toxic waste off The Netherlands, against the large-scale killing of kangaroos; at the same time whaling and nuclear testing were still accorded high priority. An increasingly characteristic feature of campaign work was the audacious publicity stunt. Scaffolding around both Big Ben and the Statue of Liberty was used to hang banners declaring opposition to nuclear testing. A line of volunteers dangled from ropes off a bridge across the Rhine to halt river traffic and to draw attention to water pollution. Perhaps most famous amongst these protests was the co-ordinated climbing of eight smokestacks on the same morning in April 1984 in Austria, Belgium, Czechoslovakia, Denmark, FRG, France, The Netherlands and the UK. Each large yellow banner displayed one huge capital letter and an anti-acid-rain slogan. Between them, the banners spelled out 'Stop Stop'. This campaign showed courage in penetrating the then uncompromising Czechoslovakia and cleverly indicated the international nature of the problem of acidic gases. Moreover, since it depended on international media coverage to have the message compiled, it indicated that Greenpeace was now confident of its celebrity and newsworthiness. Clearly, by 1984, Greenpeace was well co-ordinated and had a high degree of self-confidence.

The following year witnessed a particularly decisive incident. The *Rainbow Warrior* arrived in Auckland, planning to renew the anti-French protests around Moruroa Atoll. While it was moored in New Zealand, a diver secured two bombs to the hull. They exploded around midnight, some minutes apart, and a Greenpeace photographer was drowned as water flooded in (see Bornstein, 1988). Those responsible for actually placing the explosives rapidly left New Zealand but two French military personnel were arrested and convicted of manslaughter for their part in the plot. The prisoners were held in New Zealand but relations between France and New Zealand subsequently deteriorated, with France introducing obstacles to New Zealand's foreign trade. In July 1986 the two prisoners were transferred to military 'detention' on a French Pacific island while, in return, France called off the trade restrictions and offered compensation to the New Zealand government (Brown and May 1989, p. 135). Although the killing and the pragmatic attitude adopted by the French were a blow to Greenpeace, the events won it huge publicity and great sympathy. According to Brown and May, 'The bombing of the *Rainbow Warrior* transformed the organization, making it headline news around the world and reminding everyone of the forces that are arrayed against it' (1989, p. 5).

Since 1985 Greenpeace has grown dramatically. Greenpeace UK put the worldwide membership at the end of 1989 at around three and a half million, including the 270,000 in the UK. Its recent policies have reflected the early emphases: campaigns against nuclear weapons and nuclear power, against habitat and wildlife destruction and protection for the seas and atmosphere. It has focused on the Antarctic and on pollution of the North Sea, which involved Greenpeace groups throughout Europe lobbying their governments.

While early protests focused on almost incontestable issues, such as the dangers of nuclear testing in the atmosphere, subsequent campaigns have required more scientific evidence. Thus, Greenpeace now boasts of having the 'most sophisticated mobile laboratory in Europe' (Brown and May 1989, p. 150). While its fund-raising and recruitment advertisements still display endearing seals or majestic whales, it increasingly supports this appeal with detailed scientific and technical advice. An oblique testimony to its apparent increase in sophistication comes from a BBC Radio 4 reporter who commented, on air, with a wondering tone that Greenpeace campaigners 'now add scientific references to their press releases' (14 November 1989). Greenpeace UK appointed a director of science in 1989, a geologist with experience in seismic, and hence nuclear, monitoring. According to *The Times Higher Education Supplement* (7 April 1989, p. 8), 'much of [his] work will turn on using his university contacts to commission the right consultants, and keep up the quality of the resulting reports'.

This appears to be a sensitive issue for Greenpeace for, in the Introduction to Brown and May's volume (1989, p. 5) we learn that

> there is a current media cliché that Greenpeace is turning its back on such tactics [as direct action] and is becoming a more

bureaucratic, softer version of its earlier radical self. This is demonstrably untrue; the number of direct actions continues in an upward spiral.

These authors are insistent that Greenpeace still represents the 'rainbow warriors' of the green movement, non-violent but daring and implacable. Its commitment to direct action does continue. The fact that Greenpeace has been so successful in public fund-raising and in increasing its membership means that it enjoys a real independence from government, greater than that of the RSPB. But the trend towards growing professionalism is developing at the same time, and is achieving new kinds of recognition for the organization. At the end of 1989 it was invited on to an official scientific and technical advisory body in Belgium in preparation for an inter-governmental, ministerial conference on the North Sea (*Sunday News* 17 December 1989, p. 10). Such formal recognition is inevitably a slightly mixed blessing. Official bodies thrive on compromise and, as its recognition increases, Greenpeace is likely to face similar dilemmas to those confronting the RSNC in its relationship with the Nature Conservancy Council and the Department of the Environment.

Of the three groups surveyed, Greenpeace most fully illustrates the role of campaigning organizations as moral entrepreneurs. It has pioneered methods for environmental protesting and has very successfully brought its protests to public attention through the media. Greenpeace now has considerable power to place environmental issues on the public agenda. A roundabout acknowledgement of this power comes from those, like North (1987),[6] who suggest that Greenpeace has begun to act irresponsibly by focusing attention on rather idiosyncratic targets. To use the terms introduced at the start of this chapter, Greenpeace now has the ability to put forward social problem claims of a high initial plausibility, almost irrespective of how real the threat is. This ability is enhanced by the fact that many of the threats with which it is concerned are either intangible (such as that from nuclear discharges) or remote from everyday experience (like whaling practices far out in the ocean). Where the public has no independent access to the truth, but has only the two sides' conflicting accounts to go on, it is increasingly likely to accept Greenpeace's account.

MAKING SOCIAL PROBLEM CLAIMS
ABOUT THE ENVIRONMENT

In each of the above cases we have seen how the groups can reasonably be characterized as engaged in making social problem claims: for example, that birds are being subjected to intolerable treatment in the name of fashion; that the Antarctic is being despoiled because officials at bases, free from scrutiny, are being careless; or that because no systematic check is kept on habitat types, valuable wildlife sites are disappearing throughout the UK. There are many other environmental organizations, even just within the UK, and they have this character too. Thus, Friends of the Earth led the campaign about the use of CFCs and the danger they posed to the ozone layer. The Marine Conservation Society campaigns for the protection of marine habitats. There are bat groups, badger groups, and plant life groups. There are regionally specific groups, such as that concerned to raise money for rain forests in Belize. As Lowe and Goyder indicated, the diversity of these organizations means that one cannot readily generalize about them. For example, although a large membership is usually beneficial, we have seen how the SPNC profited from its smallness under the specific political circumstances of wartime. However, an adherence to the social problems viewpoint does allow us to identify certain features which contribute to pressure groups' campaigning successes.

Among the most important of these is the public profile of the issue. Sometimes an issue may have a high profile because it is near at hand but, as with the ozone layer, this is by no means always the case. The profile is built up by skilful campaigning. For example Greenpeace makes spectacular news: it takes filming equipment to make sure that news footage is available. In his analysis of the media, Gandy refers to this strategy as an 'information subsidy' (1982, pp. 61–2). That is, if groups can 'lay on' news in a way that saves work for reporters, that increases the paper's or the station's response to the issue. Programme makers will often be glad to make use of striking, high quality film from Greenpeace or of photo-opportunities furnished by the RSPB. Furthermore, new ways of campaigning, new events and the involvement of celebrities help to make an issue a success, irrespective of its 'objective' status. For example, the presence of Brigitte Bardot on a protest against seal hunting was important in alerting the French media to Greenpeace's environmental work (Brown and May 1989, pp. 49–50).

The impact of an environmental issue will as readily be affected by the place it occupies in the wider culture. At least within British culture, and probably much more widely, it would be easier to interest people in a threat to birds than in endangered slugs, even if the objective position of the latter were much worse. Of course, the 'popular' status of animals or other natural phenomena is subject to negotiation and change: tigers have been rehabilitated from wild killers to majestic, endangered cats, and with this change many hunters have turned gamekeepers. But the general point still stands.

The fortunes of campaigns are also affected by constraints, in particular the total amount of support available. To some extent at least, green groups have to compete with each other for members, funds, sponsors and even air-time. While the pool of potential support is quite flexible – many people will join several environmental organizations – and the competition is therefore not cut-throat, there is a contest for the highest profile and for the highest rate of recruitment. As I have already mentioned, in 1990 both Friends of the Earth and the RSNC targeted peatlands in one of their campaigns. And, as with any other market situation, there are beneficial and adverse consequences to such competition. Roughly speaking, on the benefits side there is the impulse to be innovative, to devise new campaign strategies and targets. On the other hand, several groups are likely to be attracted to what are perceived to be the most popular campaign themes; consequently the market reinforces the tendency for relatively unpopular issues to be marginalized. Such issues are nobody's favourite campaign topics even if the organizations privately regard them as important.

Two other significant features of environmental social problems emerge from these three case-studies. The first is the role played by scientific knowledge and scientific authority in making social problem claims. From the outset, scientific authority was important to the standing of the SPNR. It was the scientific credentials of many of its representatives which helped it in its negotiations with government. Similarly, we have noted the growing importance of scientific expertise in Greenpeace's arguments and the recent appointment of scientific staff. Much the same would hold for Friends of the Earth. Finally, in the case of the RSPB it will be recalled that studies of bird behaviour and bird habitats have assumed increasing importance. These examples take us back to Kitsuse and Spector's arguments about the objective aspects of social problem claims. It might well be suggested that if a social problem claim rests on sound scientific evidence then it will be more robust than those claims supported only by opinion. This is an important issue and one to which we shall return in Chapter 4, when the overall role of scientific authority in the green case is assessed.

The second aspect is the part played by government policy. The role of direct government involvement has featured a number of times: from the reversal of US nuclear testing policies to the adoption of the SPNR's proposals by the wartime British administration. But government policies play a pervasive role in less direct ways too. The significance for the various trusts making up the RSNC of job creation schemes – operated in one form or another throughout the 1980s – has already been mentioned. Other charitable bodies engaged in environmental work and which have worked on projects accepted by central or local government have received funding too. In the next chapter we shall investigate the benefits politicians obtain from such deals. But here it is important simply to make the point that such schemes can significantly alter the environment within which the voluntary groups compete with each other. Those well positioned to take advantage of government schemes, because they are close to the establishment or because they undertake work which the government would otherwise have to do itself, are likely to benefit far more than others.

It is clear that the government can exert a good deal of indirect influence over the context in which environmental pressure groups work. Other official agencies as well as firms and businesses can also have a large impact on the way in which social problems claims are made. It is therefore time to examine changes in the social context within which environmental groups operate; this is the theme of Chapter 3.

NOTES

1 It is inevitably difficult to come up with an 'objective' problem which everyone 'ought' to worry about but which is largely ignored. Most of the examples I can think of have been drawn to my attention by the media or a pressure group and have therefore not truly been ignored. However, at the risk of anticipating the rest of this chapter, arguments about the destruction of the ozone layer do appear to have fitted this pattern well until very recently.

2 The issue of membership is a difficult one. Most societies now offer a family membership option. The question then arises, how many members are represented by a family? Clearly, societies have an interest in suggesting that their memberships are as large as possible and, usually, larger than another society's.

3 Apart from the published literature dealing with the RSPB, I have drawn on a BBC Radio 4 programme about the society in the series 'Pillars of Society', presented by Simon Jenkins and broadcast on 3 December 1989.

4 Ian Prestt's interpretation was offered in his talk, 'RSPB centenary review', at the RSPB/IWC (Irish Wildbird Conservancy) conference in Belfast, 11 March 1989.

5 Indeed, far from conserving *all* individual birds, the RSPB sometimes has to cull gulls which threaten the rarer terns.

6 Richard North's views were further elaborated in an interview he gave in Simon Jenkins's programme (see note 3) and in a Radio 4 documentary he made about Greenpeace, broadcast on 6 December 1989 and entitled 'The Zero Option'.

CHAPTER 3

Green publics, green politics, green companies?

INTRODUCTION

We saw in Chapter 2 how, for many years, the green case was put forward and the green agenda was shaped by pressure groups and the environmental lobby. They publicized the environmental message and organized a few thousand people to act on nature's behalf. But they were not simply neutral agents working to meet environmental needs; they shaped the issues as well as publicizing them. The purpose of this chapter is to examine the other actors whose influence is being felt: the public, alerted and probably worried about issues publicized by the pressure groups; political organizations, responding to the public mood and to the practical demands of certain environmental problems; and commercial bodies, stimulated by public interest and the opportunities afforded by the green wave.

EXPLAINING THE 'GREENING' OF PUBLIC OPINION

The message of the social problems approach is that public opinion is largely malleable. Issues are brought to the public's attention by moral entrepreneurs; views are 'sold' and 'merchandized'. Successful groups, ones which manage to get their message aired and which find ways of attracting funds, effectively define what the problems are. In contrast to this emphasis on the malleability of public perceptions, there is a widespread tendency to think of public opinion as an autonomous force. Changes in public opinion may, for example, upset even the most carefully planned election campaign. Equally, the views of individual members of the public may be critically affected by events or problems in which no group appears to have an institutional interest. We need to ask, therefore, how green has the public become and how can their greening be explained?

We have already encountered information that is important in answering these questions. That there has been some greening of the public can hardly be denied since, as I have mentioned, the UK's Green Party received an unprecedentedly high vote in the 1989 European elections and since groups such as the RSPB and Greenpeace have continued to experience high rates of membership growth. A more direct measure of public interest comes from surveys of public opinion. In September 1989 the British Department of the Environment (DoE) presented the results of a questionnaire survey it had commissioned from the polling organization NOP; it dealt with public attitudes to the environment (Vaus 1989, p. 10). Among other things, the survey sought to find out what people regarded as the most important problem that the government should be tackling. Its results suggested that environmental and pollution problems were second only to issues of health and social services; both issues were nominated by around one third of the sample. Notably, rather fewer people (around a quarter) deemed unemployment to be the leading problem.

On the face of it, therefore, by the end of the 1980s the British public was alerted to and concerned about environmental problems. Of course, opinions expressed in surveys and polls are notoriously difficult to interpret. People may say what they believe the interviewer wishes to hear. And there is a big difference between stating that some issue causes you anxiety and actually changing your behaviour in response to that anxiety, for example by sorting your waste or by using your car less often. We may be led to take a sceptical view of expressed public opinions by the finding that as early as 1985, 66 per cent of respondents had told the Gallup pollsters that they were at least fairly concerned about global warming (Heald and Wybrow 1986, p. 150); this is one of the issues on which environmental groups would claim that least public action has occurred.

All the same, we can have some confidence in the 1989 survey because people were asked to rank their concerns. Respondents had to nominate the things which worried them most; they could not claim to be concerned about everything. In the corresponding DoE survey for 1986 only 8 per cent of respondents had put environmental and pollution issues at the top. Thus, in three years the number putting green issues first had nearly quadrupled.

How then can this greening be explained? As we have seen, many sociologists would ascribe these changes to the work of groups making claims about social problems. But there are alternative interpretations. One influential school of thought attributes these changes of opinion to major shifts in value systems. Analysts in this tradition tend to speak of 'post-materialist values' or a 'new environmental paradigm' (Milbrath, 1984, p. 14). They claim that there is growing support for new policies and politics which reflect these changed values. In essence their argument is that, for increasing numbers of people in the First World, reasonable material wants are now satisfied. Citizens can begin to concern themselves with desires for less tangible satisfactions.

This notion was originally formulated in the 1970s, primarily with respect to intangible political 'goods', such as civil liberties and political participation. The idea of a switch to post-materialist values therefore substantially predates the current green wave. Since the value change appears to have been underway for several years in advance of rising green awareness, and since in survey work 'post-materialist' values seem to be correlated with various indices of environmental concern, a number of analysts have concluded that post-materialism is the cause of the greening of the public (for a review see Lowe and Rüdig 1986, pp. 515–17). On this view, in Rootes' words (1990, p. 7), it is now

> the Green movement which has seized the imagination of those who hanker after political change ... [T]he 'green wave' is said to be about to engulf the advanced societies and the

tea-leaves are again being read for signs of the fundamental transformation of political systems.

For some writers in this vein the green movement simply happens to be the latest vehicle for post-materialist sentiment. For others it represents the logical fulfilment of post-materialist philosophy, extending 'rights' and political participation to animals and plants, even the planet itself (see the essays in Elliot and Gare 1983 and Dobson 1990). The term 'deep ecology' has been coined to refer to radical green thinking along these lines.

The green case's appeal at the level of ideas or ideology – what Rootes terms the green movement's 'moral principle' – is very significant. Lowe and Rüdig (1986, p. 537), for example, draw attention to the ecology movement's peculiarly 'inclusive' character. By this they mean its ability, largely due to the flexibility and wide scope of its ideas, to incorporate other key elements of protest movements, for instance the peace movement and various youth movements.

But strength at the level of ideas is seldom enough to account for the social and political success of a movement. Some social scientists have sought to explain its appeal by looking at groups whose interests the green movement furthers. It has been proposed (for example by Bürklin 1983, cited in Lowe and Rüdig 1986, p. 522) that the green movement coincides with the interests of those engaged in the welfare and regulatory systems of the modern state (see also Cotgrove 1982, pp. 93–7 and Cotgrove and Duff 1980, 1981). If realized, the movement's objectives would represent an increase in the social influence and importance of these occupational groups. Other analysts have adopted a 'rational choice' approach, seeking to determine what benefits individuals derive from their support for ecologism. The leading idea here is that support for ecologism can be anticipated from those who benefit more from this ideology than from other social philosophies.

However, as Lowe and Rüdig convincingly argue (1986, pp. 522–4), this calculus is hard to accept. For one thing a group's interests are hard to specify. Thus, if the most extreme environmental predictions are correct and we are all going to perish because of global warming, it is in nearly everybody's interests to support green reforms. Also, within any occupational group or class, there will inevitably be differences in individuals' beliefs, interpretations and situations. Not all civil servants or teachers would benefit equally from green reforms; nor would this benefit depend simply on the exact nature of their jobs since it would also vary with their age and life expectancy, the location of their homes, features of their families and so on. Equally important, people do sometimes act in accordance with principles which are not apparently reducible to their self-interest. Finally, approaches which treat green attitudes as a mere sub-species of post-materialist values tend to overlook two things: the specifically environmental aspects of green attitudes and the particular events (and their social and political contexts) which prompt people to take an interest in green issues.

These last two points are the most important; they are also related. Whilst 'inclusive' environmental sentiments may fit readily with other anti-establishment causes, there are specific stimuli to ecological protest, particularly events such as the disaster at Chernobyl (in April 1986), food scares and environmental incidents like the huge Alaskan oil spill from the tanker, the *Exxon Valdez* (in March 1989). Rather than being borne along by value changes and post-materialist ideologies, public concern over green issues is related to external events and, frequently, to pressure groups' and the media's responses to those events. In turn, these external stimuli are likely to be taken most seriously by people who perceive them as relevant to their everyday concerns. It is not so much their class or occupational interest in an abstract sense but their very immediate, practical interest which is enrolled. The term 'nimby' (standing for 'not in my back yard') has been coined to refer to this kind of concern. For example, people may not be opposed to nuclear power in principle, but they may object to having a nuclear waste dump near their house. And this kind of concern can unite people with very different social characteristics who happen to inhabit the same region. As Lowe has observed (1989, p. 15):

> in the [1989] European elections, while the two biggest blocks of voters for the Green Party were young, first-time, mainly student voters and former Liberal supporters, the best results were achieved in southern England in areas subject to strong development pressures.

Thus, in Lowe's view, in the huge opinion poll of the European election, general political and ideological dispositions were overlain by particular, personal responses to environmental threats and problems.

While individuals or families may be beset by a range of environmentally related issues, there appear to be certain types of development which frequently lead to collective responses. Some characteristics of these developments are rather obvious. All other things being equal, large projects are likely to catalyse action since they disturb many people at once. Yet while motorways will disturb large numbers of people, those people are socially and geographically dispersed. Airports, large factories and nuclear power plants on the other hand are concentrated. The last of these, as well as some factories, are additionally associated with insidious dangers, even occasional catastrophes. It is not surprising therefore that nuclear power plants have been rallying points for environmental action and 'politicization' throughout almost the whole of the First World (see Urwin 1990, p. 152).[1] The green ideology as has been noted may be an inclusive one; even more strikingly inclusive have been the alliances formed to oppose the siting of nuclear installations.

In his comparative review of nuclear policy and protest in France, West Germany, the UK and the USA, Rüdig notes the general pattern of alliances between local residents or working people (though not necessarily the working class), the traditional nature conservation groups, more radical environmental organizations and representatives of the 'new left' (1986, pp. 378–80). The nature of the anti-nuclear opposition is further affected by factors specific to each case; for example, the protest is likely to be increased if the proposed site is perceived as threatening a major local economic activity, if the local population is large and concentrated, and if the local people share a common sense of identity which is at odds with the metropolitan political culture. Thus, in the French case, protest in Alsace (an area with ambivalent attitudes towards French nationality) was especially marked; indeed, throughout France 'the regionalist element in anti-nuclear opposition has been very strong' (1986, p. 372).

In part, the ability of nuclear power to stimulate environmental objections can be readily, and very practically, understood. Even though power stations are usually sited in remote areas, their presence may stimulate the opposition of farmers and those who work in the tourist industry. On top of this, remote areas tend to be appealing to wildlife and its supporters; rural retreats may also be valued by the vocal, educated middle classes. Such opposition might also be anticipated for the siting of an airport (for a study see Apter and Sawa 1984), a large industrial plant or refinery, or even a conventional power station. But in the case of nuclear power radical environmentalists and supporters of the 'new left' are likely to lend their support because of alarm over the dangers of radiation and over the industry's association with the production of nuclear weapons. In some cases this political alliance with the new left has been especially marked; as Rüdig notes (1986, p. 379),

> In Germany the New Left was not involved in any environmentalist or anti-nuclear activity before February 1975. Until then it had dismissed environmental issues as an establishment plot to divert attention from more pressing questions, but afterwards the whole of the New Left . . . took on board the nuclear issue. To some extent, this embracing of the nuclear issue was a result of the failure of the New Left's previous campaigns and of the dearth of alternative issues.

Proposals for nuclear power plants appear to possess a great ability to stimulate ecological activism and to encourage green 'awareness'. But it is important not to assume that this capacity to provoke green politicization operates automatically. Its impact varies from one country to another. Thus, as Rüdig points out, the nuclear power programme in mainland UK developed into the mid-1980s without generating the degree of opposition common in continental Europe. Neither should we assume that nuclear power's provocative action is timeless; we should not ignore changes in the technical procedures employed in the nuclear industry nor developments in the public's environmental sensitivities. Thus, despite the low levels of protest in the face of the construction of UK nuclear power plants, opposition to the proposal to test sites for their suitability for the disposal of nuclear waste was anticipated (Rüdig 1986, p. 373). These sites were to be located in areas where the nuclear industry was unfamiliar, areas selected on account of their geological features rather than their remoteness. A new stage in the nuclear industry's development could well have triggered off effective opposition in a way that the simple continuation of the building programme had not. But this potential for protest was defused by the postponement of the programme on the eve of the 1987 general election (Lowe and Flynn 1989, p. 275).

The ability to stimulate environmental protest is not limited to the nuclear industry. As people come to take environmental dangers more seriously, other processes can adopt the same characteristics. Thus there has been considerable anxiety about, and organized opposition to, plans to build toxic waste incineration plants, particularly in the wake of concerns about PCBs, one of the powerfully dangerous chemicals to be disposed of at such sites (see Elsworth 1990, pp. 345–51). While such facilities lack the military associations of nuclear installations, they do serve to combine broad environmentalists with local residents and with nature conservationists (Lowe 1988).[2]

A further important feature of toxic waste disposal, shared by nuclear wastes, is that it has a significant unavoidability. The wastes already exist. Unlike plans to erect nuclear power stations, these proposals cannot be aborted before the programme has been begun. If every region objected to nuclear power stations there would simply be no nuclear energy; yet if, as seems likely, people in each locality object to waste disposal or incineration, the government or the company is still left with a disposal problem. Moreover, where there are disposal facilities it is tempting for countries or companies to import other people's waste to dispose of at a commercial profit. Complicated negotiations can ensue, as with the threatened import of Canadian waste into the UK in 1989. After an accidental spill the Canadian authorities had imposed tough restrictions governing PCBs and it became commercially attractive to send them for disposal at a site in Wales (Elsworth 1990, p. 348). This provoked a number of demonstrations in the UK. In response to such protests, companies can claim that the importing of waste for incineration is in the nation's economic interest while objectors assert that waste which is too dangerous for other countries' citizens is too hazardous for them too. As was mentioned in Chapter 1, and as will be discussed further in Chapter 5, this issue has a particular salience for Third-World nations who may not have the power, political will, or economic muscle to resist the establishment of dumps on their land.

Organizations such as Greenpeace and Friends of the Earth are alert to the dynamics and the political implications of these issues. Officials and would-be dumpers tend to argue that the waste has to be disposed of somehow and that environmentalists should therefore act 'reasonably'. They should, for example, assist in finding the best disposal site and should hold back from joining forces with the objectors at all the sites. Wary of incorporation by the establishment and conscious of the politicizing value of such protests, the response of Greenpeace is uncompromising. In its view, since it did not create the waste, it need not assume responsibility for helping to dispose of it.[3] To be 'reasonable' in such matters would run the risk of appearing to endorse a disposal technique. And if that technique were once seen to be satisfactory to, say, Greenpeace, it would be difficult for environmentalists to oppose similar plans in the future. It might even legitimate the import of other countries' wastes. On this matter Greenpeace's policy is to oppose all disposal in order to put pressure on producers to limit their output of the materials. This strategy allows environmental campaigners to ally themselves with those operating on a purely 'nimby' basis.

To summarize, it appears that the political greening of the public has not been simply a consequence of more general value changes. Nor has greening been a property of a certain class or occupational interest group. Rather, it has arisen from a combination of the actions of organized groups making social problem claims and of the responses to particular environmental threats by less formal groups. Certain of these threats were initially able to bring together ecological activists, more conventional nature conservationists, local residents and employees, and various new left and radical political groups. Subsequently, a more comprehensive green ideology was developed which allowed ecological politics to continue in the absence of an immediate threat. Under these conditions new issues, such as toxic waste disposal, could perform the same politicizing function as had nuclear power stations. Equally, new issues, even those lacking an immediate local relevance (such as the destruction of the ozone layer or recycling), could rise to public prominence. This trend away from exclusive identification with a nuclear hazard is testified to in the DoE opinion survey mentioned earlier. When asked in 1986 about the environmental hazard which was of greatest concern, over half the respondents had nominated radioactive waste; by 1989 the spread of concerns was much more diverse, with the ozone layer and the tropical rain forests joining radioactive waste as the leading issues (Vaus 1989, p. 10).

Before leaving this subject one final point should be addressed. In his account of the catalysing role of nuclear power plants Rüdig draws attention to the pioneering part played by technically authoritative critics of the programme. He suggests that lay action on its own was insufficient, as 'Expert dissent seems to have been a necessary precondition for the emergence of serious protest in the nuclear case' (1986, p. 371). Thus, although many objectors to nuclear power were opposed to it before they heard the evidence of dissenting scientists, the statements of these scientists were important in legitimizing opposition to nuclear power. Equally important, they provided critical ammunition for the protestors to use. Further exploration of the role of scientific and technical expertise will be reserved for the next chapter.

GREEN ELECTORAL POLITICS
(i) GREEN PARTIES

Up to this point we have been concerned with the reasons for growing public interest in environmental issues. However, an additional question arises about the development of environmental party politics. The performance of the UK Green Party in the 1989 elections has already been mentioned twice, but across Western Europe and Australasia and into Eastern Europe and areas of the Third World there have been significant developments in green political groupings (for a guide see Müller-Rommel 1989 and Parkin 1989). By late 1989 there were significant numbers of greens in the parliaments of West Germany, Sweden, Italy, Belgium, Switzerland and Austria, as well as a small number in other countries such as Portugal and Australia (*Guardian* 22 September 1989, p. 21).

With the success and influence of social movement groups in the UK, there was initially a debate about the need for a green or

ecological party at all. And although the UK's greens claim to be
the oldest green party in Europe there was significant opposition
from leading environmentalists (for example, Nicholson 1987, p.
116).[4] The debate seems to have had two major axes. First, was
there enough of a political programme to the green movement
to launch a party; second, even if a coherent party political
view could be put together, would it have any real prospects
at the polls.

To begin with the latter point, it is often observed that
electoral fortunes are closely tied to the voting system. Thus, in a
largely two party, first-past-the-post system – as in Great Britain
and essentially in the USA – small parties stand little chance,
whatever their political orientation. In parliaments which typically consist of alliances between small parties, as in Italy,
the prospects appear greater. In 1989 there were 22 greens
in the Italian parliament, and none in either the UK or the
USA (*Guardian* 22 September 1989, p. 21). Yet as Lowe and
Rüdig point out (1986, p. 535) parties do not seem to follow
this logic in their foundation; 'the world's first two green parties
were set up in countries with "first-past-the-post" systems –
New Zealand and Britain'. In these cases, one might say, the
parties were established more in hope than in expectation.
On the other hand, some green parties may form for quite
rational reasons irrespective of their objectively poor chances
at the polls. The French greens, again confounded by the electoral system, formed a political organization, at least in part,
because there was little other way of attaining media attention
(Lowe 1988).

The most well known of all the green parties are '*die Grünen*'
of West Germany. The party had enjoyed considerable success,
having substantially the most vocal green representation in a
national parliament and sharing in the influential city government of West Berlin. As Rootes explains (1990, p. 11), its success
does not necessarily follow from exceptionally widespread environmentalism in the German population; it is due to several
features of the complex electoral system. Elections run on a
modified form of proportional representation in which voters
have two votes, one in a constituency and one for a party list,
and where parties must pass a 5 per cent threshold in order to
gain representation. However, once this threshold is reached, the

party becomes eligible for substantial financial support from the state. Rootes observes that

> all of these factors have been reflected in the rise of the Greens: they first entered the parliamentary arena and gained national prominence by winning just 5 per cent [the qualifying figure] of the vote in the smallest state (Bremen), all of their MPs have been elected by the 'second vote' rather than in constituency contests, the fragility of their surplus over the 5 per cent threshold has been a disincentive to splinter groups, despite serious doctrinal differences, and the party receives considerably more of its income from the state than it does from its members (1990, p. 11).

Conspicuous electoral success can go hand in hand with the finding that the party's following 'is not really growing beyond its established stock of between 8 and 9 per cent of the vote' (*Guardian* 22 September 1989, p. 21).

Much has been made of the 'doctrinal differences' to which Rootes refers. They arise not necessarily because greens are particularly quarrelsome but because of the difficulties in trying to elaborate a new and comprehensive political stance. All the time that green activists only form pressure groups, or occupy only the margins of politics, they are not obliged to provide a comprehensive programme of social and economic policies. Once they aim to enter the political arena with any electoral credibility they face a testing time from other parties, the media and putative supporters. This was the essence of the debate over the viability of green party politics.

In their study of groups making social problem claims Kitsuse and Spector (1981, p. 203) asserted that such groups

> may transform themselves into genuine political parties if they fail to gain satisfaction from the existing regime. In doing so, however, their specific 'social problems' are likely to be lost or transformed by intra-and inter-organizational political processes and concerns.

These authors' observation about the transformations which movements undergo when they become party political is aptly borne out in the case of the UK green party. We can begin with a review of the party's practical concerns. Formed in 1973 (and then called PEOPLE), the party first came to wide public attention as a result of the decision to field fifty-three candidates in the 1979 general election. This number was of crucial importance since only those parties contesting over fifty seats were entitled to election broadcasts on television and radio (Parkin 1989, p. 221). While this brought the party valuable publicity (and in fact a greater share of the vote than in either the 1983 or the 1987 general election), it was an expensive exercise and nearly exhausted the organization's finances. Equally, although the publicity attracted many new members, it overstretched the group's administrative resources. The organizational consequences of this move into widespread electoral contests took many years to sort through; the party stayed small and prone to in-fighting (Rüdig and Lowe 1986). After the disappointment of the 1987 general election, the 1989 success in the European contest was enormously important. Still, even that brought problems. The small staff was almost overwhelmed by the administrative demands of the rising membership. The party was relieved not to lose any of its deposits but the campaign still cost an estimated £97,000, which is hard to recover solely through subscriptions (*The Independent* 22 January 1990, p. 2). This financial burden has led to some post-electoral impatience from members; as its press officer stated to the *Guardian* 'Our members are always complaining we are not in the news any more, but quite honestly if we are going to react to events as Britain's third biggest party, we've got to have some money' (*Guardian* 1 February 1990 p. 6).

But the problem is not simply one of money. As a would-be major party they also face problems in policy formulation. These can usefully be seen as of two sorts: first, immediate policy measures to ensure the party's growth and, second, the elaboration of green politics. The first of these was particularly prominent at the 1989 party conference. The UK greens recognize that they are disadvantaged by the electoral system. There is accordingly a strongly felt need to seek electoral reform. Sara Parkin, the party's 'international liaison secretary', proposed a motion under which the Greens would enter into a pre-electoral pact with the other opposition parties to place just one candidate in each constituency (*The Independent* 25 September 1989, p. 4). Duly elected, if all went to plan, this anti-Conservative alliance would form a government, introduce proportional representation, and then immediately dissolve Parliament. In the ensuing general election all parties would be free to return to competing with each other. The motion did not meet with success, falling well short of the required majority. There were several reasons for this failure, for example a belief that the Greens should be offering a full green manifesto. But there was also anxiety about the pragmatic political behaviour which the pact would have necessitated; many in the party are wary of compromising with the 'old politics' of the established parties and fear that inter-party deals are undemocratic.

Such internal disagreements over strategy and politics are usually described as a split between a pragmatic tendency and an uncompromising wing; adopting the terms applied to *die Grünen*, these trends are often dubbed 'reali' and 'fundi'. This split should not be over-emphasized. Members and supporters do not necessarily fall into one category or the other. Importantly, the party has a clear, and widely accepted core of policy commitments: to a unilateral anti-nuclear stance, to stringent limitations on pollution, to a decrease in economic inequalities, to the decentralization of economic and political power, to limitations on overseas trade – which, because of transport costs, is seen as inherently wasteful – and to a reduction of the population to a sustainable level (Byrne 1989, pp. 104–7). It is, however, in the elaboration of these policy commitments and in strategic decisions that the differences emerge.

For one thing, members disagree about how exacting the party can afford to be about the sponsors it accepts (*Guardian* 1 February 1990, p. 6). As will be seen later on, many companies are keen to be perceived as green and are willing to sponsor organizations in return for a flattering association. The Green Party knows it needs money, but it is hard to decide exactly whose funds to accept. Similarly, the exact details of income redistribution are difficult to work out. Should proposals be the ones which are 'greenest' (whatever precisely that means) or ones which are easier to 'sell' to the electorate? As party members actually acquire political power (as *die Grünen* have found) these decisions become harder. Also, as the UK Greens become more credible they are subjected to sharper scrutiny by the (frequently) right-leaning press. At the 1989 party conference, it was feared that participants would be outnumbered by journalists. Even the *Guardian*'s representative found much to mock, including plans to collect (and recycle) human excrement, a discussion of the contraceptive benefits of cannabis use, and a workshop called 'Rearing Your Green Child' (23 September 1989, p. 4). Any internal differences were liable to be taken up and gleefully pursued by journalists.

Overall, the UK Green Party benefits from the fact that it can look to the policies and practices of more electorally successful European greens. The European greens collaborate closely, with *die Grünen* even going so far as to redistribute some of their (state-derived) financial resources to harder pressed colleagues. Yet, the UK Greens have not been able to sustain their position as third-largest party in the polls. By early 1990, with the Labour Party benefiting from the unpopularity of the government's 'poll tax' and of continued high interest rates, the Greens' support had fallen to around 4 per cent and they had slipped behind the Liberal Democrats in the polls (*The Observer* 25 February 1990, p. 1). In general these poll findings were borne out in the by-elections of the first half of 1990.

GREEN ELECTORAL POLITICS
(ii)   THE GREENING OF OTHER PARTIES

If the future for the UK Green Party looks difficult, and even that of *die Grünen* not spectacularly good, it might still be argued that these parties' importance lies in the effect they have had on the other major political groups. The large green vote in 1989 might be interpreted as a trigger to bring about the transformation of the dominant British parties.

Certainly, after the 1989 elections the other parties in the UK quickly saw the dramatic appeal of greenery and acted to make themselves appear greener. The Conservative administration, for example, brought Chris Patten — who had a reputation for sensitivity and environmental sympathies — to head the

Department of the Environment. By the time of the Green Party Conference in September 1989, Sara Parkin was ready to satirize the other parties' new claims to be the real greens:

> have you ever heard the Labour Party say that it is the real Conservative Party? Or the Conservatives claim to be [Liberal Democrats]? What is it that makes us the party that everyone else want to be? The answer is very simple. We are right and they know it. (*Guardian* 22 September 1989, p. 6)

Though it may be flattering to have your adversaries wishing to impersonate you, there is a danger that – in the voters' eyes – they will succeed. In Britain the two leading parties have been busy seeking to improve their own green ratings and to undermine the green aspirations of the other.

Party spokespersons and allied authors have tended to argue along two lines. Critics of the Conservatives have generally proposed either that free-market conservatism is inherently incapable of serious greening or that the Conservatives are irreformable in practical terms. The flavour of the first of these arguments can be represented by the following summary provided by Lowe (1989, p. 17); the claim is that the Conservatives' 'commitment to privatization, deregulation, rolling back the state and the morality of the market is antithetical to a vision of government as the enlightened guardian of the environment'. While this commitment may not be equally distributed through the whole of the Conservative Party, it does resonate with the ideology of Margaret Thatcher and her closest supporters. Still, the Conservatives have fought back on this point, arguing that the market is just the kind of sensitive system needed to handle environmental judgements, and citing the growing power of green consumerism (see below). They can even point to the encouragement of the use of unleaded petrol through a pricing advantage as evidence that the government is willing to take the necessary steps to help the market go green. This market-led approach is enshrined in the *Blueprint for a Green Economy* (Pearce, Markandya and Barbier 1989), a carefully argued document suggesting that environmentally benign behaviour can to a large extent be encouraged through free choices in a market in which the pricing system has been adjusted to account for environmental impacts. This document is exerting considerable influence at the DoE (see Cope 1989a).

This line of in-principle criticism is most commonly levelled at right-wing parties. But it is important to note that Labour has not been exempt from this criticism either. The failure of command economies in Eastern Europe to avoid great environmental damage would seem to imply that state agencies may be poor at anticipating environmental needs too (see Buerk 1989). So, while some authors have suggested that 'Empirically and logically, new politics is [sic] related to some aspects of traditional left-wing policies' (Poguntke 1989, p. 181), the argument is not as decisively in favour of Labour as many commentators appear to think. All the same, at the in-principle level Labour appears to enjoy some advantage. It is far from clear that *all* environmental issues can be handled through market mechanisms. And left-wing governments are more at ease with the necessary degree of regulation than their right-leaning counterparts.

The second line of argument deals with practicalities. Again starting with the Conservative side, the claim is that the party's main political supporters – industrialists and traders – have an economic interest in avoiding the costs of environmental measures and that there will always be a resulting strain between their private interests and the state's actions in the interests of the environment. Thus, in February 1990 Chris Patten was reported to be facing opposition from cabinet colleagues who did not wish to see their particular responsibilities hampered by the costs of greening. The supposed clashes included environmental regulations which made oil exploration off Scotland more costly; misgivings about the expansion of the road network and car ownership; and air pollution controls which would increase the cost of cleaning emissions from power stations (*Guardian* 24 February 1990, p. 7).

Yet, here again, Labour's position faces difficulties too. Historically, it is committed to improving the lot of its working-class supporters. Consistently with its non-revolutionary political stance, this objective has been approached through encouraging economic growth, supplemented with only a little redistribution of wealth. It is difficult to reconcile this traditional commitment to increasing the nation's output (especially in those sectors which provide working-class jobs) with its present need to address the environmental issues which might attract the middle-class supporters it needs to get back into power. It is unclear how to do both at the same time. In Rootes's judgement, 'it was precisely this dilemma that plagued the German [social democrats] and allowed the Greens the space to develop' (1990, p. 8).

Overall, therefore, both leading parties, if not incapable of profound greening, are likely to have difficulties in finding the will to do it. It is on the strength of this realization that Lowe and Rüdig argue that the green ideology has a curiously 'exclusive' character (matching its inclusiveness, described above). Deep down, it resists assimilation by the traditional parties (1986, p. 537). Some critics would take this point further and argue that capitalist production is inherently antithetical to true ecologism (see the tradition represented by Bosquet 1977, pp. 173–92). For such authors the inability of West European parties of right and left to turn bright green is no surprise, since none of them seeks to abandon capitalist mixed economies. This point of view is similar to that adopted by some environmentalists allied to 'deep' ecology; it will be considered later on in this chapter.

Of course party politics are much more than contests of ideas and principles. And environmental issues can become embroiled in the practicalities of inter-party competition. That some environmental measures can be adopted for rather un-green reasons is nicely illustrated in the following case of local government politics. According to Wainwright (1989), in late 1989 opponents of the Conservative council in Bradford found themselves outflanked. The council had voted funds for four new environmental projects, not all – according to opposition spokespersons – of first-class quality. Among the victims of this re-direction of spending were community organizations previously funded by the council but hostile to its Tory controllers. Wainwright quotes the leader of the local Liberal Democrats as saying, 'The Tories clearly wanted to get rid of the money so that it wasn't there to spend on other things.' Opposition politicians wished to attack this change in funding but they could ill afford to be seen as hostile to 'green' schemes (whatever their actual quality). In the context of party politics it is this moral unassailability of green measures which allows them to be used for political expediency. Green expenditure 'gild[s] the final grants list with worthiness' (1989). The spur to political support for environmental action may have next to nothing to do with politicians' actual conversion to greening.

Cope (1989b, p. 8) describes a further episode which illustrates this point, in this case in connection with environmental labelling. 'Eco-labelling', the official designation of certain products as environmentally benign, is a growing trend and will be discussed below. But Cope observes that while right-wing governments are generally disinclined to support such initiatives, since they involve government expenditure, the UK 'government is strongly promoting the idea that a European Community-wide' scheme be introduced. He suggests that this is because the UK government is keen that there should be no barriers to trade after the inception of the single European market in 1992. If countries each have their own labelling system this could lead to obstacles to trade; the UK government is thus attracted to a pan-European scheme primarily for economic reasons. Once again politicians are being led to espouse green causes for non-green motivations. Although the two cases cited here concern the actions of right-wing politicians, this expedient use of greenery is not confined to one end of the political spectrum.

THE GREEN MOVEMENT AND GREEN POLITICS

The large number of votes won by the UK Green Party in 1989 was almost as encouraging for the green movement as it was for the party itself. But the party and the movement are far from identical, and the comparative success of the party has rendered their differences much clearer. For one thing, it led the pressure groups to distance themselves publicly from particular party associations. Addressing the Green Party Conference in 1989, Jonathon Porritt – at that time director of the UK Friends of the Earth – was reported as having warned his audience that 'the Green movement, including Friends of the Earth, would never specifically endorse the Green Party. All the pressure groups which made up the movement were dependent on being politically independent' (*Guardian* 23 September 1989, p. 24).

This message had been very clearly spelled out to FOE volunteers in the *Local Groups Newsletter* in the month after the European election; they must not open themselves to the accusation that they endorsed particular parties or candidates. This emphasis on party political neutrality is not new to FOE; as Rüdig points out, FOE refused to participate in a UK anti-nuclear campaign, formed in 1979 by environmentalists, trade unions and political parties, precisely because it was an 'outrightly political organization involving political parties' (1986, p. 398). Environmental groups do not wish to run the risk of becoming subordinated to party politics. For one thing, in legal terms their charitable status (adopted by most, though not all, groups (Allaby 1989, p. 150)) obliges them to limit their political commitments. Nor can they afford to alienate potential members who happen to vote for some other party; according to Benton (1989, p. 11), 15 per cent of members of FOE are Conservative voters.

The second point is that the green movement benefits from a flexibility denied to the Green Party. The former can concentrate on specific issues at certain times without the need to have a policy on a broad front. It is also spared many of the administrative burdens and costs of a political party. It is free to pursue its campaigning objectives wherever an opportunity presents itself. Thus, in December 1989 Jonathon Porritt made news when it was revealed that he had had a private meeting with Margaret Thatcher (*The Independent* 11 December 1989, p. 2).[5]

The third significant feature of the distance between the green movement and the Green Party is that it allows each of them to avoid criticisms aimed at the other. The greens' success was followed by the almost inevitable backlash. *The Independent* (4 August 1989, p. 10) referred to the 'Stalins of greenery', keen to order everyone around in the name of the planet's needs. Peregrine Worsthorne, in the *Sunday Telegraph* (20 August 1989, p. 19), argued: 'Just as red extremists did their best to stop capitalism solving the problems of mass pauperization . . . so there is a danger today that extreme greens might stop capitalism solving the environmental problem.' There were elements in the rhetoric of the Green Party – elements much played up by their critics in the Conservative Party – which appeared authoritarian. If you sincerely believe that you know what the world needs, it is easy to become impatient with those who fail to agree with you. As Paastale (1989, p. 84) reports, among the greens in Finland there was a proposal 'that Finland should be transformed into a one-party state where the only party allowed would be a green vanguard party'. This suggestion failed to grasp the public's imagination, but it does hint at the moral and political certainty which can flow from believing yourself to be the earth's saviour. While green totalitarianism is extremely unlikely, the separation of the movement from the party helps to shield the movement from such allegations.[6]

ENVIRONMENTALISM AND CAPITALISM
(i)   THE GREEN SELL

So far we have looked at public opinion and at the political reaction to greenery. Another important element in the recent response to environmentalism has been at the level of commerce and trading. The idea that ordinary people can affect the environment through their purchasing decisions has become very popular; it is a direct way in which people who might not necessarily join a pressure group or the Green Party can participate in the green wave. Some advocates of green consumerism have viewed it very positively; Richard Adams of the consumers' magazine *New Consumer* gave full voice to this interpretation when, at the 1989 Green Party Conference, he was recorded as saying that 'The shopping centre was the polling station and the cash till was the ballot box' (*Guardian* 22 September 1989, p. 6). In the UK, best-selling books have been published on how to become a green consumer and a green capitalist (for example, Elkington and Hailes 1988 and Elkington and Burke 1987; see also Button 1989) and leading papers and magazines have been quick to respond to this line of thinking by running their own 'green shopper' features.

As we saw in the Introduction, companies and their advertising consultants have been adroit in their response to the perceived requirements of the green consumer. For example, during

1989, rival UK supermarkets ran full-page newspaper advertisements boasting of their haste in banishing CFCs from their new warehouse-cooling systems and of the environmentally-friendly practices of the farms from which their food was obtained. Some companies, as we also saw, made false or exaggerated claims. The green sell could easily degenerate into a 'green con'. In some cases this was no doubt attributable just to carelessness and over-enthusiasm on the part of advertisers. Elsewhere it appeared more cynical. For example, many supermarkets began to stock washing powders which were free of phosphates and which were promoted on these grounds. (Phosphates are one of the constituents of washing powders which are discharged with the waste water and which can lead to biological damage through excessive enrichment of rivers and water courses.) These products sold well and all too soon they were joined by washing-up liquids which also declared that they were phosphate-free. Yet phosphates had never been added to washing-up liquids in the first place. There was no environmentally relevant difference between these liquids and ones which did not carry the phosphate-free slogan (*Guardian* 8 September 1989, p. 27). The slogan was truthful, but the greenness was illusory.

Environmental campaigners were equally dismayed by manufacturers of recycled toilet tissue. Several of the leading producers had already been using recycled paper prior to the green wave. But they had not advertised this fact, feeling that customers preferred the notion that toilet tissues were wholly new and hygienic. Once recycling became fashionable, it was easy to re-label these products without changing the manufacturers' practices. Early in 1990, FOE campaigned to persuade manufacturers to recycle low-grade paper for toilet tissue rather than employ the high-grade waste which is in common use but which could – with greater environmental benefit – be substituted for virgin wood in the manufacture of stationery and other products (FOE 1989). According to FOE, manufacturers could do better than simply recycle; they could recycle in a discriminating way.

In all, the effect of green consumerism is difficult to evaluate. While it has been used by virtually all environmental pressure groups (after all, even the RSPB's original anti-feather campaign was consumer-based), and while specific campaigns have met with resounding success (for example in 1990, the anti-fur campaigners were heartened by the closure of Harrod's fur department),[7] there is a widespread fear that the 'bandwagon effect which is associated with green consumerism is a very mixed blessing' (Irvine 1989, p. 3). Companies will stress only those aspects of their work which appear green and consumers, happy that they are doing something for the environment, will not inquire too deeply. Among companies, the response to green consumerism is likely to be an attempt to make the easiest and cheapest environmental improvements to their products and to take their reforms only as far as is necessary to retain their market share. Indeed, in a programme on green consumerism broadcast on BBC television, an advertising agency's report to companies about the need for a green image was quoted.[8] According to this report

> There is no reason to give up in despair if your product is environmentally-unfriendly on two dozen different counts . . . Consumers, journalists and (mainstream) pressure groups are still all implicitly accepting piecemeal progress – so long as the company concerned appears to have a genuine commitment to moving in the right direction.

Cynicism is not as rampant as this report implies. And there are limits to pressure groups' 'implicit acceptance'. As Irvine points out (1989, p. 4),

> In its recent advertising, we are informed that 'Green Meanz Heinz'. The company is, for example, paying £1m for a 'Guardians of the Countryside' Conservation Programme in association with the World Wide Fund for Nature. But it had to drop its £75,000 sponsorship of Green Shopping Day, in September 1989 when its links with the massacre of dolphins through tuna fishing were exposed.

If a company seeks to capitalize on its green image in an explicit way it opens itself to embarrassment at the hands of investigative environmentalists. In such cases, once a company has started to proclaim its green character, it may have to become progressively greener. Thus, on balance, green consumerism is likely to benefit the environment. But in some cases it will also lead attention away from, even legitimate, the retention of environmentally damaging practices at some stage of the manufacturing process.

In the first rush of enthusiasm for environmentally benign products, manufacturers scrambled to apply 'environmentally friendly' labels. A 'Babel' of claims to be the friend of the environment ensued. Environmentalists feared the consequences of this confusion of claims, for even when they were not misleading, they were not standardized. The favoured response to this is a system of eco-labelling. Here again the West Germans lead. Since 1978 they have been operating the 'Blue Angel' system under which there is a standard stamp for environmentally benign products. In addition, around the edge of the stamp is a short explanation of why the label has been granted – for example, because the product biodegrades rapidly (Cope 1989b, p. 9).

Although this system attracted praise for its pioneering role, environmentalists began to criticize its detailed operation. Originally the label concerned only the environmental status of the parts with which the consumer came into touch, rather than the whole life history of the product. So, if a factory caused a lot of pollution but its product did not, this product could still qualify for the label. Pressure groups are now demanding a cradle-to-grave system which pays attention to the production process, packaging and ultimate disposal. Some firms have been quick to respond to this new approach and, like the motor manufacturers Volvo and Saab, have begun to stress the durability of their products and the extent to which environmental considerations inform the whole production process.

However, there are problems inherent in this proposal. For one thing it makes the labelling process more complex, costly and (probably) time consuming. Moreover, it is extremely difficult to draw a boundary around the factors which should be counted in. Effluent from the production process would no doubt count, but as Cope observes, it is hard to know whether the fact that the product arrives at the shops in a truck rather than by rail should lead to its disqualification. Equally it is tricky to decide how wide the boundary can be. It is hard to imagine how any car – even the most fuel-efficient – could receive the label but should all 'bicycles qualify for labels because compared with cars they are less polluting?' (Cope 1989b, p. 9). Finally, environmentalists are concerned that even a labelling system can be used cynically. For example, manufacturers are likely to change their procedures in only those areas which lead to the granting of the eco-label; they will then perform the rest of the manufacture as economically as possible rather than as harmlessly as possible.

The green consumer has clearly had some effect on existing traders. But he or she has also provided altogether new opportunities. Some of these have been relatively trivial, as with the *Rainbow Warrior* computer game launched in association with Greenpeace (*New Consumer* autumn 1989, p. 29). A far larger and more influential market is afforded by green investment funds. Developing the existing idea of 'ethical investments' (investments in companies which, for example, avoided military connections and which refused to trade with South Africa), some firms began to offer 'green funds' from the mid-1980s. In the USA, by 1989 such funds were estimated to be worth about $150 billion (Schwarz, 1989b). Once people with savings are willing to delegate their green financial decision-making to investment specialists, these funds can become very powerful corporate green consumers. In many cases these funds have also performed well, if only because the firms they back tend to have anticipated the tightening of environmental regulations.

The 'greening' of finance and of business also provides environmentalists with opportunities for income generation. We have already seen that some of the RSNC's wildlife trusts have established environmental consultancies as a way of generating revenue. Before long, such groups may well be offering to perform 'eco-audits' for firms. For a fee they will assess a firm's conduct, for example by analysing their recycling policy, their energy efficiency, their purchasing policy and so on. Firms which implement the groups' recommendations would be able to feature an endorsement by the environmental organization in their advertising. Greening will be allied with public relations, and environmental groups will receive financial benefits.

The same logic applies to individuals who act as environmental consultants. There is an increasing number of people able to make a good living in this field (Vidal 1990). Companies wish to avoid making costly environmental errors and also to avoid adverse publicity. Famous and authoritative environmentalists can command high fees (which they often pass on to environmental projects) for such advice. But dangers lurk here. In defence of their trade, such consultants tend to argue that companies are bound to develop new plants, processes and buildings. It is therefore better to offer some advice than to let the companies push ahead in ignorance. Others fear that consultants are used to give a green hue to developments that are basically environmentally unsound. The public will be reassured and criticism will be forestalled. Worse, it is currently an unregulated profession. There are no agreed qualifications for being an environmental consultant nor agreed criteria for environmental assessments. Still, the profession is here to stay; the most realistic goal for which environmental campaigners can press is agreed, and increasingly stringent, assessment criteria and greater freedom of information.

Among those he interviewed, Vidal cites one critic of such consultancies who asserted that environmentalism 'is about saving the planet, industry is about making a profit and the two do not mix' (1990). The green sell inevitably brings the green movement into close touch with commerce and industry, and accentuates the difference between those greens who believe that the capitalist mixed economy can be reformed and those who believe there must be profound changes in the entire socioeconomic order. In carrying out their day-to-day business, most sections of the green movement avoid taking a hard line on this question, preferring to treat environmental issues in a pragmatic way. This strategy prevents differences of policy emerging and avoids the risk of alienating supporters. However, green parties are beginning to have to declare their hand; in particular, as we have seen, the UK Greens have had to combat right-wingers' claims that they are crypto-Stalinists.

This issue can be expected to increase in importance, although there are already some signs of tension. While advocates of change through green consumerism embrace the reform programme, they face some strong opposition: in response to a planned Green Shopping Day in 1989, some environmental activists were reported as favouring a no-shopping day (*Guardian* 28 September 1989, p. 3). Some aim to convert capitalism; others seek to renounce it.

ENVIRONMENTALISM AND CAPITALISM
(ii) CONTRADICTIONS?

At present there is a more or less pragmatic agreement to accept green consumerism. For some greens it marks the onset of a wealthy yet sustainable economy. For others it is the earliest recognition that our economic activities must change profoundly. In 1988 Jonathon Porritt wrote that he was 'depressed' to find that FOE was held to be 'the only environmental organisation "which argued that green growth is logically impossible"' (1988, p. 22). He was depressed not because FOE endorsed this view, but because next to nobody else did. In his view, this shows that the 'vast majority of UK environmental groups ... have been co-opted by the growthist [sic] obsessions of our industrial culture'.

A similar argument had, for some years, exercised an attraction for certain neo-Marxists. They claimed that 'Capitalism, either private or State-operated, is incompatible with human survival' (Bosquet 1977, p. 173; see also Caldwell 1977). Because of its inherently competitive character, the capitalist economic system continually needs to grow. To produce only as much as last year is to lose out to your competitors who will be trying to produce ever more. For many decades now, inspired by this competitive impulse, modern capitalism has been producing more and more. This has created plenty in much of the Western world; in fact most reasonably affluent people now have more food, clothes and possessions than they could readily justify. The capitalist system succeeds by convincing us that we want or need further, new goods. But for Bosquet the crucial point is that while growth is *attractive* to the consumer, it is *essential* to the economic system.

This imperative has several consequences, among them that manufacturers have been tempted to make things which wear out in order to ensure a future market.[9] This impulse leads to waste and to environmental damage. But even more ecologically harmful is the constantly increasing drain on raw materials. For example, the motor industry succeeds by selling us more and more cars; consequently, we deplete our metal and oil resources ever more quickly. For Bosquet, the 'dynamic' of capitalism drives us towards ecological disaster. And it does so irreformably.

Deep greens, including Jonathon Porritt, would accept much of this analysis. For them, though, the culprit is industrialism rather than capitalism *per se*. This is partly a practical point; they see no reason to be soft on socialism when the ecological problems created by industrialization in the Soviet Union and Eastern Europe are fearsome. Indeed, in most respects industrialization under 'state socialism' has been more environmentally damaging than under capitalism. This is especially true when such damage is considered in relation to economic productivity: command economies have delivered less wealth for an equivalent environmental cost (see the reports in *Time* 9 April 1990, pp. 24–32). But deep greens' objections also stem from a belief that current levels of consumption are in any case too high to be truly sustainable, so that even a radical redistribution of wealth would not solve the problem of dwindling resources. At this point the argument between the new left and deep greens can become rather tortuous. A lot hangs, for example, on whether the pre-Gorbachev Soviet Union is interpreted as having been 'state capitalism' or some form of socialism. The greens are rather silent about the political forces which could bring about a self-denying retreat from 'industrial materialism' (Porritt 1988, p. 23). For their part, eco-socialists are unclear about why socialist materialism would be any better – sufficiently so as to save the planet – but they do agree, that far-reaching economic regulation is necessary.

For the West's green parties it is a matter of political urgency to present a view on this question. And they are torn, since they have to put forward their ideas in a competitive political forum in which they must appear green enough to make a real difference but run the risk of losing support if they seem to offer economic hardships. The Department of the Environment survey, mentioned earlier on, suggests a growing public awareness of these issues. For example, very few respondents (6 per cent) accepted the proposition that 'Development of the economy should take priority over questions of the environment' (Vaus 1989, p. 11). Of course, this does not tell us exactly how self-denying people are prepared to be when it is their own economic well-being which is at issue.

Of late the UK greens have been cautious in stating their position on this issue. At the 1989 conference, David Spaven, one of the party's speakers, was quoted as saying 'we are not a no-growth party. We are not an anti-technology party' (*The Independent* 25 September 1989, p. 4). Similarly, in an interview with *The Independent* (21 September 1989, p. 8), Sara Parkin had claimed:

> We're looking for circular economic models where you have the minimum input per unit of production, and as much as possible goes round and back to where it started, so that there is minimum waste and pollution. You would measure success – you can call it growth, if you like – by how little you put into it, and how little you waste.

Such claims are not mere evasion. As Pezzey (1989) argued in response to Porritt, 'green growth is logically possible'. It is logically possible to heat people's homes better than before and still use less energy. It is logically possible to improve urban transport and yet produce fewer greenhouse gases. More energy-efficient techniques create these possibilities. And supporters of mixed-economy solutions argue that technical innovations are much more likely in a regulated but still formally free market than in a planned economy.

The market is an efficient means of getting goods and services to people who want them. But the market is also inherently wasteful. Alongside commercial successes there are inevitably market failures and these consume energy and materials to no practical advantage. In that narrow sense capitalism and environmentalism are contradictory. There can be no capitalism without waste. But it is an open question whether innovative capitalism coupled with regulations on market freedoms (for example, obligations to recycle or lighter taxation on more benign products) can be more efficient than ecologically-minded command economies. At present, the capitalist West looks environmentally far superior to the state-dominated East. However, as we will see in Chapter 5 this may be because some of the environmental costs of the West's wealth are borne by the Third World, whereas the Soviet Union, for example, has to a larger extent felt the effect of its own drive for industrialization. While it is important to note that the question is open, we are unlikely to see the answer tested in practical terms in the near

future because of the current counter-reaction to state socialism
– a counter-reaction spurred by command economies' failure to
produce plenty rather than by their dirtiness.

INTERNATIONAL GREEN POLITICS:
THE CASE OF ACID RAIN

International comparisons in politics are of great importance. It
is ironic therefore that much debate on environmental politics
has been conducted within national parameters. In some cases
practical reasons prompt this restriction. Pressure groups commonly work within a national context since they are dealing
with the legal framework which prevails in a particular country
and because they can get to know the leading politicians, civil
servants and media personnel. Similarly, because of national
electoral systems, green parties have tended to be founded on
a national basis. Even critics of capitalism have tended to offer
their analyses in terms of the single country they know best.
This national trend is doubly ironic if one takes into account the
fact, pointed out in Chapter 1, that many, if not the majority of
environmental problems are international in extent. Increasingly,
environmental organizations and national governments are having to operate in an international context. The case of acid rain
can stand as an example of this kind of issue.

The debate over acid rain was introduced in Chapter 1.
In essence, in the early 1970s it was noted that woods and
aquatic life in Scandinavian countries were beginning to suffer from the effects of acidification. Their environmentalists
blamed much of this on the emissions from power stations
and factories in other countries, notably the UK. Little acidification was detected in Britain itself and the government, the
(state-owned) generating authority (the CEGB) and the (state-
owned) coal industry – which supplied much of the power
stations' fuel – were inclined to argue that evidence for the
connection was weak and inconclusive. On top of this, the
steps which Britain was being urged to take in order to reduce
acidic emissions from power stations were expensive. It was
argued that the government had a responsibility to the tax-
payer to be sure that emission controls would bring benefits

worth the expense before they took any action (Irwin 1990, pp. 16–17).

Several features complicated the development of this debate. For one thing, the technical issues involved were enormously complex (Irwin 1990, pp. 6–8). The exact chemistry of acid rain was hard to investigate. There were often irregularities in the timing of peaks of acidification so that correlations between effects and supposed causes were hard to draw. Finally, the effects themselves were enormously variable, seeming to depend on details of local geology, climate and vegetation (Schoon 1990). This technical complexity provided sceptics with plenty of opportunity for saying that the causes of acidification were not understood but that they would act just as soon as conclusive evidence was available. Furthermore, it was an act of faith which allowed the government's adversaries to argue that acid rain from UK power stations definitely was the cause of Scandinavia's environmental problems. The matter was further complicated because the UK government was ideologically committed to reductions in public spending and thus ill-disposed to spending on emission controls. It was also keen to privatize state industries and did not wish to see the electricity industry encumbered with future environmental regulations.

However, during the mid-1980s more comprehensive scientific evidence was beginning to be collected and the government found itself under pressure from official and 'establishment' scientists, from certain MPs who championed environmental issues, from pressure groups and increasingly from unified foreign governments. Some distance between the government and the CEGB emerged (Irwin 1990, pp. 17–19). European governments were calling for the UK to join them in a phased reduction in acid emissions. Initially the UK did not reject the principle but objected to the precise conditions. For example, it argued that the 1980 baseline, against which reductions were to be measured, was unfair to Britain because its emissions had already fallen in the late 1970s. The Europeans countered that the earlier fall had not been a planned reduction; rather it was the consequence of Britain's recession and industrial decline and thus a reduction which would be quickly cancelled out once recovery set in. From December 1983 officials in the European Community had been working on the details of a directive which would govern this phasing out. But by the time it was adopted in 1988 it had been significantly modified. Some countries, including the UK, had pressed hard for the reductions to be lessened. These negotiations served both to reduce the directive's severity and to consume time before it was actually implemented. International agreements nearly always have this quality of compromise. Although technical information is important to the decision-making its influence is mostly indirect (see Collingridge and Douglas 1984; also Lindblom 1980). Agreements, as they are euphemistically called, are usually the result of prolonged trading.

International agreements are going to be an increasing feature of environmental politics, particularly in Europe, where national governments can be overridden in many respects by EC directives. But international policy making is likely to be adversarial and to stem from compromise, not necessarily from the best understanding of the needs of the environment:

> this 'internationalization' also means that questions of the environment may become inextricably linked with wider international bargaining over monetary relations or diplomatic disputes . . . the present international political and economic order may impede the implementation of environmentally-sound development strategies. (Irwin 1990, p. 26)

CONCLUSION

In this chapter we have reviewed the greening of public opinion, of political parties and of commerce and industry. We have also looked at the factors which have shaped the way that this greening has taken place. For example, where sections of the public have begun to take action for environmental causes, they have often done so because of perceived personal threats. By and large, political parties have been prompted to accommodate to environmental demands either by successful lobbying or because of competition from other parties. And it has been the combination of commercial pressures, lobbying and legislation which has been responsible for what greening there has been in industry.

In consequence the greening of different countries has so far proceeded in very different ways. The UK's parliamentary system does not encourage great political flexibility; none the less, certain environmental pressure groups have developed access to the centralized power of Whitehall and Westminster. They have been very successful in setting the agenda for conservation policy. Elsewhere in Europe, party competition from the Greens has been more influential. But the very openness which offered the Greens the chance of parliamentary representation in those countries means that the role of lobbyists is less significant there. In the near future, international politics will be of increasing importance in affecting legislation and in bringing more uniformity to states' policies. It is significant that leading pressure groups are already operating on an international basis, reflecting in many cases the cross-national character of environmental problems.

The effects of greening have been patchy within countries also. As has been mentioned, there are regional trends in the public concern about environmental issues. But there are class differences too. Up until now, it is mostly wealthier consumers who have taken part in, or benefited from, the greening of products. Typically, it is the more expensive cars which have catalytic converters and it is better-off shoppers who can afford to buy according to 'greenness' rather than price (for example, in the choice of organic vegetables). It is only to be expected that greening under capitalism will produce such patterns. This realization is seized on by critics of capitalism but, in the present world political climate, even ecological arguments will not revive the fortunes of state socialist planning.

It is important to note also that, although some of the benefits of green consumerism accrue directly to the purchaser (as with healthier food), in other cases (as with catalytic converters) the benefit is more widely distributed. As we have seen, there are even pressures to take the environmental assessment of products back into the manufacturing process. Moves in this direction will have strong implications for workplace conditions and thus for the health and well-being of the working-class population. (By extension, there will also be direct implications for those people of Third-World countries who work in mines, factories, or plantations that supply the First World; see Chapter 5). The unresolved question is, how far can pressure groups succeed in bringing about large changes in producers' practices, either through campaigning for legal reforms or through altering consumers' attitudes? A key resource they bring to this task is scientific evidence for the urgency of environmental problems. In the next chapter we turn to an examination of the character and the role of these scientific arguments.

NOTES

1 In relation to the subsequent discussion of green parties it is worth noting at this stage that, in a 1984 poll of UK Green Party members, 44 per cent of respondents belonged to CND while FOE had only 21 per cent, see Parkin 1989, p. 216. Current figures would, no doubt, be very different but this poll seems to testify to the galvanizing effect of the nuclear issue.

2 In her study of the development of green politics in the Irish Republic Baker (1990) makes the point that plans for a centralized toxic waste incinerator are expected to create just these problems. Significantly, in putting forward her argument she considers Ireland's environmental problems in relation to its dependent economic status, in that, for example, it is the host to many foreign transnational companies and also has encouraged mining operations. In her view, therefore, it shares environmental problems characteristic of many Third-World nations (see also Allen 1990). This issue of the relationship between environment and economic dependency will be explored further in Chapter 5.

3 In Richard North's documentary on BBC Radio 4 entitled 'The Zero Option', broadcast on 6 December 1989, a Greenpeace spokesperson said 'For us it's a victory any time that something like that happens, that a disposal option is cut off because that is another warning back to the producers to say, don't generate that waste any more.'

4 Nicholson regards party political activity as ill-advised. In his view, only political naïvety would lead people to adopt this strategy: 'In the hands of the naïve [the expansion of environmentalism] has sometimes led to direct entry into the political arena' (1987, p. 116).

5 Although the meeting was not publicized in advance, news of its having occurred was later 'leaked'. The news suited both sides, emphasizing FOE's credibility in the highest circles while reflecting favourably on the Conservatives' claims to be taking green issues seriously.

6 There has also been sporadic concern about the possible growth of 'green terrorism', with violence being used to protect nature's perceived interests, see *The Independent on Sunday* 22 April 1990, p. 17.

7 It was reported on BBC Radio 4 News on 21 April 1990 that the final closure of the department was marked by a large sale. The store is also maintaining its fur-storing facility for those whose garments need to be kept under special conditions.

8 The programme, entitled 'The Green Sell', was broadcast on BBC2 on 6 December 1989.

9 In their recent advertising Saab, the Swedish motor manufacturer, has boasted of its environmental friendliness. Alongside the usual claims about lead-free petrol and catalytic converters, the advertisement notes that the cars' component parts are all marked with identifying codes so that parts can be re-used. Clearly, this offers to make recycling of second-hand parts much simpler and takes the 'greening' of the car further than most manufacturers do. But, even if this practice were to be adopted widely, its viability depends on models continuing to be in production for prolonged periods. New, 'improved' models will generally require many new components. Consumer goods can lead to waste by being allowed to become technically obsolete as well as by wearing out.

CHAPTER 4

The science of saving the planet

INTRODUCTION:
GREEN AMBIVALENCE ABOUT SCIENCE

Brown rice and sandals do not amount to a cure. That much is suspected by most people now worried about the dangers threatening our environment. If we are to diagnose the worst ailments from which the planet is suffering, and to treat them successfully, it stands to reason that our approach must be informed by scientific understanding.

This quotation and the chapter heading are taken from an editorial in *The Independent* (25 September 1989, p. 20). They bear witness to the central claim of this chapter: that the green movement is peculiarly dependent on science. But this dependence is no simple matter and my purpose is now to explore the practical complications which surround it.

We have already encountered a good deal of evidence for the close relationship between science and the green movement. This relationship may take many forms. Thus, in Chapter 1 we noticed Margaret Thatcher's call for scientific studies of the greenhouse effect and her decision to find funding for research on global temperature change. She insisted that environmental policies must be based on sound science. We noted also (in Chapters 1 and 3) that the international dispute over the responsibility for acid rain had technical as well as political dimensions and that the evidence of scientific experts has been very influential in shaping legislative measures to limit acid emissions. In Chapter 2 we saw how the RSNC had grown through

its scientific interest in nature and wildlife; we observed also
that official nature conservation practice in the UK, following
the RSNC's lead, was based on the notion of sites of *scientific*
interest (see Lowe 1983). Today also, the constituent bodies of
the RSNC, the wildlife trusts, generate funding and publicity
through scientific work, especially through consultancy services.
Even Greenpeace, the rainbow warriors, were proud of their
scientific expertise and boasted about their mobile laboratory
or 'action bus'.

It seems we might join with Nicholson (1987, p. 81) and
claim that conservation 'should be science led and science based'.
But there are two important grounds for being hesitant about
such aspirations. For one thing, many of our environmental
problems originate in the scientific and technological nature of
our civilization. In many instances the connection is clear and
direct. Humans invented the CFCs that are threatening the ozone
layer. Technological advance allowed humans to develop nuclear
power, which in turn has brought us persistent environmental
problems, such as those associated with the calamitous explosion
at Chernobyl in 1986. In such cases we can trace environmental
problems directly to specific products of science and technology.
There is also a more diffuse connection: present-day industrial
society is inseparable from pollution caused by motor vehicles,
power generation and waste disposal. Many environmentalists
are thus critical of technical progress and at least ambivalent
about science.

The second reason that environmentalists are loathe to grant
science a leading role is that, on closer inspection, scientific
expertise soon begins to lose its straightforward appeal. For
one thing, in many disputes over environmental policy, scientists are aligned on both sides. We have already seen that
there may be disagreements between experts over standards
of food safety or in their assessments of the risk associated
with toxic waste materials. And, although the nuclear industry
depends on very high levels of scientific skill and draws support
from many eminent scientists, we saw that Rüdig regarded the
role of dissenting scientists in the anti-nuclear movement as
particularly influential. The industry has its scientific critics
as well as its scientific advocates. As we shall see, there can
be various reasons for disagreements among scientific experts.

Sometimes the relevant evidence is simply hard to obtain or there may be a range of scientific information which has to be taken into account. In such cases scientists would not necessarily be expected to agree. On other occasions lay persons may suspect that the scientists associated with a corporation or industry are not acting in a truly impartial way.

To find that scientific evidence, far from being an impartial resource for resolving a dispute, may become part of a pressure group's campaign armoury takes us back to the social problems approach described in Chapter 2. Analysts of social problems suggested that the correctness of social problem claims was comparatively *un*important in determining their public impact. If scientific truths can be matters of dispute – particularly among experts – then even support from science may afford only a limited influence on behalf of those making claims about social problems. If we accept this point then it is harder to view the environmental movement as science led and science based in any simple way. We can usefully begin our investigation of the peculiar scientific dependence of the green case by comparing environmentalists' arguments with those of other campaigning groups.

THE GREEN CASE AND SCIENTIFIC AUTHORITY

Despite the fact that, unlike many preceding social movements, the environmental movement claims a scientific basis, little attention has been focused on the particular role played by its scientific credentials. Such a claimed basis is not unique; movements for the adoption of scientific medicine and for public hygiene, for example, share it. And, of course, the label 'scientific' is itself open to negotiation and extension, so that movements dedicated to preparing a welcome for visitors from outer space or to the promotion of a biblically based Creation Science might be heralded as scientific, at least by their supporters (Wallis 1985). But the green case is profoundly a scientific case.

Amongst its strongest planks is the argument that disaster for the human race is a natural inevitability if certain practices continue: if we persist in allowing CFCs to escape into the atmosphere, if we cut further into the world's rain forests, and if we do not reduce the emission of greenhouse gases. Other arguments concern not our survival or even the perpetuation of our current standard of living. They concern the damage to the world's other inhabitants: the need to protect wildlife by not bleaching nappies with chlorine, by conserving endangered habitats, and by not using detergents which are rich in phosphatic water softeners.

While, as we have seen, each of these arguments is now beginning to command public attention, it is important to appreciate the extent to which they are all based in a distinctively scientific perception of the world. Thus, to take the most dramatic example, the ozone layer is only available as an object of knowledge because of our scientific culture. At ground level, ozone is relatively uncommon and remote from experience. The stratosphere where it is prevalent is even more remote. Knowledge about the hole in the ozone layer is only available through high-technology ventures into the atmosphere high over the poles. Similarly, our everyday supposition is that detergents have done their job once they have left our washing machines or sinks. We would not readily think of the damage they might be doing in streams and rivers. It is biological scientists who detail the connection between water-softening agents and the algal blooms which choke life out of the water courses. Finally, there are occasions when environmental damage is done by massed products of which each of us uses only a little. It takes an unusual turn of mind to total the amount of leachate from apparently innocuous rubbish tips or to work out that many millions of tonnes of carbon dioxide are being pumped out from car exhausts. Ordinary members of our culture would have no conception of what even a tonne of gas was like.

Thus, the green case is tied to science. It states that natural realities constrain our options in various ways. Moreover, these constraints are relatively independent of people's moral standpoint. By this I mean to contrast the greens' arguments with the motivating concerns of other social movements such as the dispute about abortion and the right to life. Although 'life' itself has the appearance of a scientific notion, and scientific evidence is brought to bear in the debate (for example, to ascertain when the various bodily organs in the foetus start to function), scientists are generally reluctant to pronounce on the point at which life begins. They commonly present this as a metaphysical rather than a scientific issue. Additional moral arguments are also brought to bear during this debate; for example, it is often argued that, if 'pro-lifers' are serious in their convictions, then they should be campaigning with equal vigour for more help for AIDS sufferers or for those in Third-World countries who are struggling with life-threatening problems.

To take another example, we can return to the case of campaigns against 'too much' sex and violence on television. The claims about exposure to too much sex are typically made in moral terms. Freedom of artistic expression is weighed against moral propriety. Of course there is an empirical aspect to this dispute. Campaigners may assert that – as a matter of fact – 'over-exposure' to licentious material leads to moral degeneracy. But such claims have proved very resistant to empirical test; degeneracy, for example, is itself a morally charged notion and thus hard to measure in an agreed way. Furthermore, those interested in the debate often call on their personal experiences to assess the validity of the competing 'factual' claims and are reluctant to hand the matter over to those, such as psychologists or media analysts, who claim to have disinterested expertise.

By contrast with these social problem issues, environmentalists would see their case as unanswerable by virtue of its scientific credentials. The ozone layer *is* disappearing and the consequence *will be* greater amounts of damaging radiation; greenhouse gases *are* accumulating and a consequence *will be* the expansion of oceanic waters and associated flooding. These are held to be matters of fact and there is little room for moral dispute about them.

Many conservationists see their case as motivated, in Moore's words (1987, p. xviii), by 'objective reasoning'. Moore, who was a leading scientific authority in the Nature Conservancy/NCC until his retirement in the mid-1980s, relates how he was able to establish that toxic pesticides accumulated in the food chain (1987, pp. 157–66). It was not a question of opinion; he had demonstrated that through unexpected but relentless natural processes, farming practices were threatening to poison people. The scientific demonstrability of the connection was decisive. Max Nicholson, the leading environmentalist who has been mentioned already in connection with the RSNC and the Nature Conservancy, makes the same point. Again speaking

of the organochlorine insecticides, though this time in relation to attempts to persuade the agrochemicals industry to
change its policy, he states, 'Had not the scientific base of
ecology and conservation been already so sound, the successful
agreement with the industry could not have been concluded'
(1987, p. 49).

Moore and Nicholson suggest that the scientific credentials
of the conservation movement lent it considerable authority.
This claim can usefully be understood in relation to Weber's
famous analysis of the social bases of authority. Weber identified
three kinds of authority: the traditional, the charismatic and the
legal-rational (1964, pp. 328–9). In his view, claims to authority
may be made on the basis of hallowed and accepted wisdom. Or
they may be made on the grounds of the personal authority of a
special leader, deity, or prophet. Or they may be made imperson-
ally, on the basis of accepted and demonstrable principles. Weber
argued that the last of these, legal-rational authority, increasingly
pervades contemporary society. According to scientific conservationists such as Moore and Nicholson, it appears that the
environmental movement is peculiar in its commitment to such
authority. Other social and political movements commonly draw
on traditional authority (for example, nationalism), charismatic
authority (new spiritual movements) or on some combination
of these.

However, environmentalism's connection to science is not
simply a question of *current* authority and expertise. It is not
simply a matter of the inherent quality of scientific knowledge
(in other words, a matter of epistemology). The connection is
also made at the level of historical association. Many of the more
'establishment' nature conservation societies have a background
in natural history: the RSNC, the British Trust for Ornithology,
the various Naturalists Field Clubs and so on (see Sheail 1976,
pp. 48–53; 1987). Scientific views and scientific authority have
been central to their organizational development, as Nicholson
remarks (1987, pp. 91–2):

> While parallel movements such as those for development and
> the relief of poverty in the Third World, or for peace and
> disarmament, have had to create their own often sketchy
> foundations, environmental conservation differs in resting

upon a comprehensive and profound set prepared for it in advance by the natural history movement.

On this view the green movement is doubly bound to science, by epistemological affinity and common descent.

LEGAL-RATIONAL AUTHORITY AND THE SOCIOLOGY OF SCIENCE

The special authority enjoyed by legal-rational forms of argument has often been taken for granted by social scientists. Indeed, since social science too appears to rest on this form of authority, to throw it into question might seem a self-destructive pursuit. But in the last two decades there has been a reassessment of this kind of authority among sociologists and philosophers of science who have studied decision-making in what might be taken to be the temple of legal-rational thinking, natural science. What they have suggested is that the authority commonly associated with scientific beliefs is not as straightforward or as unequivocal as many people, including Weber, appear to have assumed (see Barnes 1985, pp. 72–89; Yearley 1988, pp. 16–43). These sociologists and philosophers have argued that the public, policy makers and more traditional philosophers of science have exaggerated the authority of science. Essentially, there are two components to this claim. First, they argue that scientists' judgements inevitably go beyond the evidence on which they are based, so that scientific authority cannot be justified by a simple appeal to its factual foundations. Second, they argue that even the facts themselves on which science is based do not command an unquestionable authority.

Let us start with the status of facts. Our confidence in the ability of facts to validate scientific beliefs often draws support from an analogy with perception. Facts are often taken to be evident in the same way that the things we see are evident; we are passive recipients of knowledge in the same way as we receive the evidence of our eyes. However, this analogy ironically works to undermine the case that it is supposed to support, since perception is far from the passive operation that this argument implies. To observe is to do far more than merely allow one's retinas to be bombarded with light since objects which are 'seen' as being the same may actually present very different appearances to the eye.

For example, as sunlight is reduced by a passing cloud, the colour and appearance of objects – as measured, for example, by a light meter – change, yet we regard the image of objects as staying the same. Equally, we can retain a constant interpretation of an object despite approaching it from many different angles. In these ways we 'see' more than actually strikes the eye. At the same time, we use only a minute amount of the visual information potentially available at any given time. Seeing is usually the imposition of interpretative schemata on to the available information; observation is a blend of interpretation and the reception of light. The extent to which humans habitually depend on interpretation in seeing is demonstrable through such things as optical illusions and trick pictures.

Just as perceptions have to be worked at, so do observations of facts. An unskilled observer allowed to wander in a wood will experience great difficulty in 'observing' the different kinds of tree for there are likely to be as many variations between members of one species as there are between the differing types. The difficulties would be magnified if the observation were done over a protracted time period so that buds came and went, fruits appeared, or leaves fell. An experienced botanist on the other hand would not only immediately see the kinds of tree but would be able to observe higher level degrees of similarity between different species; see signs of health or disease; and see whether the season was late or early.

In putting the argument this way I am not trying to raise doubts about botanists' knowledge or expertise. But I am aiming to throw doubt on the idea that scientific knowledge is valid simply because scientists see the world *plainly*. All useful seeing is skilled seeing.

But the argument does not stop there. The status of scientific facts is even more complex than this analogy with perception reveals. Many scientific observations are made with machines: one observes an electric current or radiation from space not with one's senses but with an instrument. Similarly, 'holes' in the ozone layer cannot be seen in any straightforward manner. Their existence is inferred from detector readings obtained during flights over the poles. Scientific observations, particularly in the context of experiments, also have to be separated out from chance occurrences. A rise in sea-level due to freak weather conditions will look much like a rise due to global warming. Even scientific apparatus appears to be inhabited by gremlins, and observations of changes in a meter reading or of blips on a pen-chart have to be divided into real facts and mere artefacts. Furthermore, the frontier of things which count as factual observations tends to shift as scientific ideas change so that what, at one time, would have been regarded as hypothetical – images from a new and experimental form of microscope for example – come later to be regarded as unproblematic observations. Finally, the facts of interest to scientists are commonly not single, isolated facts but are facts about classes of things: for example, that ultra-violet radiation admitted through a hole in the ozone layer would damage plankton. In such cases it is evident that no one could have made observations on all plankton, certainly not those which are not yet living. There is, therefore, something undeniably conjectural about factual claims regarding a whole class of phenomena.

So far we have looked at scientific facts and the problems in establishing facts by observation or experiment. This focus corresponds with one facet of science; sometimes science is held up for admiration as a body of factual knowledge. Most often, though, it is theoretical knowledge which is regarded as the principal achievement of science. The expectation that the earth's temperature will rise because of the greenhouse effect is a prediction based on scientific theory. The suggestion that algal growth is encouraged by discharges from farm and domestic waste is based on theoretical understanding in biology. Sociological studies of scientific reasoning have indicated that theoretical judgements in science are not dictated by the factual evidence in any narrow sense. In part this is a logical matter. In principle at least, a set of facts can always support more than one theoretical interpretation. But also, at a practical level, it is generally impossible for scientists to collect all the information they would like before having to decide on a theoretical interpretation. Scientists' theoretical beliefs are not fully decided by the factual evidence available to them.

These issues can be illustrated by taking one of the most famous examples from the history of science: the dispute between those who believed that the sun revolved around the earth and those who held the opposite view, that the earth orbited the sun. These were rival, conflicting theories. Yet both were based on factual evidence, indeed largely on the *same* observations of the sun's apparent movement across the sky. Astronomers tried with great determination to settle the matter but factual evidence could not readily be used to adjudicate the issue. For one thing, the facts proved hard to collect because, for example, telescopes provided poor images. However, even when new information was gathered, both sides were able to adjust their theories to take account of the new data. Both sets of astronomers were able to make adjustments to the orbits which they calculated for, respectively, the sun and the earth. Although only one theory could be correct, both were based on evidence and both could plausibly be modified to accommodate new data.

This extremely sketchy account is useful for illustrating two things: first, that it is often a major practical challenge for scientists to establish what the facts are and, second, that judgement has to be used to assess theories in the light of factual evidence. Scientific theories do not adjust automatically in the face of new evidence. Indeed, theoretical developments can sometimes lead people to change their minds about previously accepted facts. After a change in theoretical perspective, things which were once seen as facts come to be regarded as having been errors of observation or of measurement.

It is important to repeat at this point that these arguments about scientific knowledge have not been introduced in order to criticize science or scientists. They have been introduced because they indicate the ways in which the acquisition of scientific knowledge is far more complex than is normally supposed. Scientific knowledge depends on judgement; therefore the environmental movement's dependence on science cannot be expected to provide greens with undisputed authority.

The abstract points made in this section can be exemplified if we turn to the case of an experimental test which was designed to address public fears about one particular environmental issue. Although this case is not necessarily typical of the role of science in environmental matters it is illustrative; it has been described in some detail by Collins (1988).

The UK atomic power industry collects spent fuel from the nation's power stations at Sellafield in Cumbria for reprocessing, that is for chemical treatment to recover usable nuclear material. The spent fuel is transported by rail in special containers mounted on flat trucks. Many environmental groups are concerned about the hazards which may result from reprocessing and they have sought to focus public attention on risks associated with the various stages in the reprocessing operation. One stage which has been highlighted has been the transport. Objectors have tried to raise doubts about the safety of the flasks in which the material is carried: what would happen if there were a collision, or a fire, or a terrorist attack?

To some extent their anxiety was shared by local authorities through whose districts the flasks were transported. By 1984 these questions were being raised insistently and the CEGB took steps to quash people's doubts. They did this by arranging an experimental test. In front of thirty-two carefully sited cameras, a remote-controlled British Rail locomotive, pulling three carriages, smashed into a 'derailed' flask and truck at 100 miles per hour (Collins 1988, pp. 731–2). The steel flask was flung into the air by the force of the impact but was subsequently seen to be substantially undamaged. The measured pressure inside had fallen by only a quarter of 1 per cent and, had it contained nuclear material, no leak would have resulted. The chairman of the CEGB, an enthusiast for nuclear power, was very pleased with the result and argued that the general public's doubts should now be dismissed. He suggested that while it might have been possible to harbour doubts about the flasks' safety when the public only had the CEGB's word for it, the results of this test should be fully convincing (1988, p. 726).

However, when interviewed by Collins, a Greenpeace representative claimed that he was unconvinced. It was not that he doubted that the flask had survived the collision, nor that the train had been travelling very fast. Rather, he argued that certain features of the test materials rendered the experiment unrealistic. For one thing, there were flasks of various designs in use. The one in the test had thick, solid steel walls while other models were composed of a thinner steel casing lined with lead.

Such a flask, he feared, might not have withstood the blow. Moreover, he claimed that the kind of locomotive chosen for the test happened to have a softer 'nose' than others in common use; accordingly, some of the force of the impact would have been absorbed by the crumpling of the locomotive rather than being transmitted to the flask.

The test was subjected to further criticism because of the arrangement of the collision. It has already been mentioned that the flask was flung into the air in the crash. This was possible because the flask was placed at the end of a section of track with a large clear space behind it. The Greenpeace spokesperson argued that this detail made the test rather too easy for the CEGB. The impact of the crash was not sustained precisely because the flask was flung aside. Very different circumstances can easily be imagined. For example, had the flask been caught between a locomotive and a hard surface (the side of a cutting or the inside of a tunnel, say) the forces on the flask would have been more intense. Greenpeace's representative suggested that such a scenario was not far-fetched; indeed, the conditions arranged by the CEGB for the test could readily be seen as less 'life-like'. As Collins remarks, 'Presumably Greenpeace would have wanted a harder-nosed locomotive, with differently weighted carriages, with the flask pressed against the abutment of a bridge at the moment of impact, thence falling from a high viaduct on to a hard surface and into a fierce fire' (1988, p. 738).

Using this example, we can return to the issue of the character of scientific knowledge. I described two important considerations which affected scientists' authority: first, that their judgements inevitably go beyond the factual evidence on which they are based and, second, that facts themselves do not enjoy an unassailable status. This case study bears out both these points.

Let us look first at the facts of the case. In the narrowest sense we can say that a specific train, travelling at a certain speed, collided with a particular flask without rupturing it. But it is not easy to progress from this rather uninformative statement. Since there are various designs of train and different types of flask, it is unclear whether we can say that flasks can withstand (high-speed) impacts from trains. The CEGB's representatives might well propose this as a 'fact', while Greenpeace spokespersons would doubt it. There is a clear photographic record of the impact but the parties continue to dispute what facts these observations support. (A photograph of the collision can be seen in Allaby's book (1989, p. 127); significantly for my present argument, the book is entitled *Green Facts*.)

This leads us to the issue of judgement. Even if the parties had agreed that the experiment showed that all nuclear flasks can withstand such impacts from all of British Rail's trains, it would still be unclear whether this collision can represent all mishaps which may befall the flasks. In other circumstances there might be an explosion or enormously high temperatures; how would the flask behave under those conditions? The question of the safety of the flask requires an act of judgement in addition to the experimental test.

As I stated earlier, there are anomalous features to this test. Scientists would never normally accept the result of just one impact. Equally, they would generally require that the flask be tested under a range of circumstances. Collins argues that although this collision looked like an experiment, it was really more of a demonstration exercise. It was designed to display the safety of the flask rather more than to test it. All the same, this case helpfully demonstrates the complexities of turning to science for the adjudication of an environmental policy problem and indicates the ways in which the authority of scientific pronouncements may be challenged. No matter how many tests there had been, Greenpeace could always have queried the 'facts' and could always have thought of novel and bizarre ways in which the flask might have been damaged but which were not covered by the experiment. It could challenge the facts and challenge the judgements which allowed general conclusions to be drawn from those facts.

PUTTING SCIENCE TO WORK FOR THE GREEN CASE

Up to this point we have looked in general terms at the part scientific arguments play in the green case and at some of the limitations which may beset scientific authority despite the respect which it normally commands. It is now time to examine the use of science in the work of environmental campaigners. Conservation and environmental organizations do make extensive use of science; they call on expertise on, for instance, food chains, on species identification, or on energy conservation. For their size, they have large numbers of scientifically trained employees. They typically have scientific advisory committees and call on the voluntary support of university scientists and scientific civil servants. As we have seen, even the more radical of them are increasingly interested in taking on scientific skills; Greenpeace has recently appointed an academically trained geologist as its new 'director of science'.

But is this scientific base sufficient to grant environmental groups the authority to which they aspire? This question can be answered by taking a look at the ways in which their scientific skills are typically 'cashed in'. The evidence presented in the following pages comes from two sources: from my two-year observation and interview study of non-governmental environmental groups in Northern Ireland[1] and from an analysis of the published literature on issues tackled by leading environmental groups. Data from the former allow us to examine how scientific expertise is used on a day-to-day basis, while material from the latter permits us to analyse the role of scientific knowledge in the more technically complex debates, for example over global warming. In both cases we will examine the difficulties in 'cashing in' on scientific authority and ask how good a friend science is to the green movement.

SCIENCE AS AN UNRELIABLE
FRIEND – EMPIRICALLY

The first way in which science is an unreliable ally is a simply empirical one. Compared to social movements which appeal to an orthodoxy or to a charismatic leader, avowedly scientific movements face a number of practical disadvantages. Scientists may not have an answer to every question. Similarly, they accept in principle that their knowledge is revocable and incomplete. This incompleteness may manifest itself in a number of ways. For example, the scientific committee of one of the groups studied, the Ulster Wildlife Trust (UWT),[2] was concerned to learn of proposals to use a quarry some thirty kilometres north of Belfast for dumping domestic refuse. At present, the principal site for domestic waste dumping in the Belfast area is the north foreshore of Belfast Lough and there is considerable anxiety about the impact of this practice. It may be damaging to the marine life in the lough and to visiting bird life; the site is also flat, open and clearly visible. Thus the prospect of having an alternative site for dumping was initially attractive. However, there were also reservations about the control which might be exercised over the leachate from the proposed quarry site, especially since the quarry was close to Larne Lough, another sheltered marine lough which is the site of an RSPB reserve. The committee members had no special expertise on the matter of leaching and did not wish to appear oppositional for the sake of it, but they were uneasy about being seen to consent to the quarry-fill. The scientific committee found itself in a rather 'counter-factual' position: while they assumed that there was an answer to the question 'which site is better', they had to acknowledge they did not know what it was.

The same problem can be even more acutely felt if there is some public pressure to announce an answer. In a recent case the same organization was invited to comment on a proposed holiday development. In this case the scientific committee of the UWT was very gratified to find that it had been consulted about plans to extend a sewerage system for a caravan park and amenity centre which happened to be close to a UWT reserve. However, it had no specific expertise on this subject and – at least in the short term – no precise way of finding out what the effects would be. It was embarrassed by its lack of knowledge in the light of the unusual invitation. To have nothing to say when specifically asked to comment seemed to contradict its claim to speak for nature's needs; but there were equal dangers to speaking without authoritative knowledge.

Although the explicit invitation to comment made this case unusual, this difficulty in responding to planning proposals is not uncommon. Often it is unclear ahead of time what the implications of a scheme will be. It is tactically unattractive to object to everything but it is hard to be seen to be condoning something which may turn out to be harmful. This position might be seen as putting scientists in the position of spoilers who are tempted to view all change as a disturbance of the natural order and to ascribe all environmental damage to human influence.

The vulnerability of environmental groups' scientists on this charge can be seen with regard to TBT, an anti-fouling preparation applied to boats and other marine equipment.[3] The use of this substance, especially in important marine areas, is opposed because it is likely to be harmful to aquatic life; under test conditions it can be shown to be associated with developmental abnormalities in shellfish. In opposing a recent plan to site a salmon farm in a sheltered marine lough in Northern Ireland, conservationists were concerned that the fish cages would need to be treated with TBT or a similar preparation. Although plainly worried by this possibility, members of the UWT's scientific committee were aware that they could not say precisely what consequences would follow from such a use of TBT. In part this was because different uses have different effects. For example, the application of anti-fouling agents to boats distributes the chemical around the lough, while the results of using it on cages would depend much more on current directions. Again the scientists were in the awkward position of assuming that there was a scientific answer to the question of the anti-foulant's effect but of acknowledging that they did not know what it was.

There is a clear feeling in the UWT, as in other groups affiliated to the RSNC, that there is a need to be 'reasonable' and not oppose all development, yet the very rigours of scientific evidence and proof render 'reasonability' very difficult. The situation is further complicated since the conservationists have an additional reason for wanting to oppose potentially harmful measures: they consider that it is harder to stop something from continuing once it has been set up than to prevent it altogether. For instance, once jobs have been created by a fish-farming project it is harder to close the operation down, even if its effects are shown to be harmful to wildlife, than not to create the jobs in the first place.

The limited and provisional nature of scientific knowledge thus makes it hard to respond satisfactorily to innovative proposals. But 'not knowing' can also be disadvantageous because of the impact it has on the public. Members of the public may look for authoritative judgements and may be dismayed by factlessness. They may look to the scientific experts in conservation organizations for the answers to questions that concern them personally and be frustrated because the 'experts' do not know. Birdwatchers, and even sportsmen, may be concerned about the reasons for fluctuations in bird populations. They see this as the kind of question which conservation scientists should be able to settle, but the scientists may well not know nor even be sure how to find out.

Science may thus be a poor ally to environmentalists because scientists find their lack of knowledge exposed. Sometimes they may lack the ability or expertise to determine something which they wish to know; at other times they may know less than the public would like them to know – unlike a traditional or charismatic authority they do not have the ability to respond to every contingency. In some measure, such 'shortcomings' may well be common to all forms of the public use of scientific expertise but the conservation scientists face these problems in a particularly concentrated way. The possibility that there are difficulties, peculiar in some way to environmental concerns, has recently been discussed by Cramer (1987). Taking five short case-studies of environmental controversy, she identified three principal reasons for the difficulties that scientists faced in these cases and that encouraged, or prevented their resolving them.

The first reason she gives is that scientists confront 'pragmatic uncertainty' which arises because they are commonly called on to make recommendations at short notice, often using readily-available research material which may be very variable in quality. They are frequently without the time or resources to conduct research of their own. Scientific equipment and research can be very expensive. Environmental groups simply do not have the financial resources to commit funds to major research projects. Even those organizations with big budgets face many conflicting demands. For example, Greenpeace's campaigns and their campaign boats continually require high levels of funding. For its part, the RSPB uses much of its income for the purchase of reserves for the direct protection of birds. To spend money on research is to divert funds from direct environmental action. In many cases environmental groups are not even able to monitor all the potentially useful scientific information which is published in journals; after all, even university libraries subscribe to only a fraction of the available scientific journals.

Cramer's second point is that environmental scientists are handicapped by theoretical uncertainty, arising 'from the low level of theoretical development of (ecosystems-)ecology' (1987, p. 50). There is less consensus in ecological science than in many other areas of natural science, so the interpretation of ecological events is likely to be disputed. We will return to this point in the next section.

The third form of uncertainty stems from the sheer complexity of large-scale phenomena taking place in open systems. This sort of difficulty has already been mentioned in the case of TBT dispersal. Environmental scientists face two sorts of disadvantage here. For one thing, unlike many other technical experts (for example in micro-electronics or robotics) they have not built the system on which they are advising. It is not a small universe over which they exercise a great deal of authority and control. Second, there are other parties who have a large say in regulating the system. For example, farmers and the Ministry of Agriculture can claim expert knowledge of food production needs which counterbalance conservationists' claims about the needs of the country's wildlife.

According to Cramer, this uncertainty and the sheer bulk of material which could be collected meant, in cases of dispute, that opposing interest groups could select information to suit their own purposes. Worse still, in Cramer's view, despite these uncertainties, the ecologists 'felt pressed to come up with clear answers ... They achieved this by evaluative steps which were largely coloured by political and ideological premises' (Cramer 1987, p. 62). That is, in her view, they adhered to a rhetoric of scientific certainty although their choice of evidence was influenced by prior ideological or commercial commitments.

There is, however, at least one sense in which Cramer's account understates the extent of uncertainty that conservation scientists face. The pragmatic uncertainties deriving from the complexity of the systems with which conservationists deal and from the sheer bulk of material available to them can be augmented by another consideration. There are some matters which are on the margins of observability. Ironically, the significance of this factor is attested to – in a roundabout manner – by Nicholson as he argues for the importance of scientific knowledge in the progress of the conservationists' case. He summarizes early conflicts between environmentalists and various established groups, such as oil-shipping concerns (which were not regulating discharges), pesticide manufacturers (who were not aware or careless of the entry of toxins into the food chain) and farmers (who were aiming to increase productivity at the cost of wildlife and habitat) (Nicholson 1987, pp. 44–53). He documents how each of these cases was fought out through argument, publicity and lobbying, and concludes by saying,

> The record shows that environmental conservation sooner or later succeeds in dealing with offences of a tangible character but recently the trend has been towards much more disturbing *intangible damage* to the environment, either through chemicals let loose to roam through different layers of the atmosphere, or through nuclear radiation. The resulting problems are particularly disturbing because they strike so widely at the roots of global life support systems, because *their agents are technically so difficult to monitor*, especially when they combine spontaneously with one another after release, and because of their ability to become transported rapidly over long distances and at varying altitudes by air currents, *whose movements are imperfectly understood* (1987, p. 54, emphases added).

Environmentalists face a practical difficulty when they have to decide how to respond to 'intangible damage' and to agents which are almost impossible to monitor.

Here again science is a less than perfect friend to environmentalists. If, for instance, the hole in the ozone layer is less pronounced one year than before, is that attributable to that year's odd climatic conditions or does it throw doubt on the trend which had hitherto been taken as proving depletion? Equally perplexing, some predictions suggest that the greenhouse effect will lead to greater variation in the weather so that cooling as well as warming could be seen as evidence for the existence of the effect. Even the interpretation of fluctuations in the numbers of migratory birds is subject to the same sorts of problems.[4] Huge flocks of birds are very difficult to monitor in detail;

if the numbers at a particular site fall for one season this may be because that local habitat is declining in quality, or it may be due to any number of other factors: harsh conditions during migration, unusual predation during breeding and so on. Admittedly, these may be extreme cases (although it is important to note that some of the leading global environmental issues number amongst them). But they do serve to make clear one central point: the empirical fallibility of science, most pronounced when phenomena are at the limits of observability, means that social problem claims founded on science must offer hostages to fortune.

CASE STUDY: SCIENCE AND THE GREENHOUSE EFFECT

I outlined the problems we can anticipate from the greenhouse effect in Chapter 1. It seems obvious that if we continue to add carbon dioxide to the atmosphere the earth will become warmer on average and then flooding and climate disruption await us. But the simplicity of this message belies the complexity of the greenhouse effect. Although we can hardly doubt that the human race discharges billions of tonnes of carbon dioxide into the atmosphere each year, we are far from certain about the fate of all the gas we discharge or about the relative significance of humans' impact on the atmosphere. While a billion tonnes (also known as a gigatonne) sounds like a huge amount, as Pearce (1989, p. 114) reminds us,

> the atmosphere contains about 700 gigatonnes of carbon; the planet's soils, forests and plant life hold a similar amount, with perhaps twice as much in soils as in plants. The sea waters hold some 40,000 gigatonnes, 60 times more than the atmosphere. So far, humans have located a mere 4,000 gigatonnes in coal and oil deposits . . . But all these reservoirs pale beside the carbon in sedimentary rock at the bottom of oceans. That total is around 70 million gigatonnes.

It is easy to see that if any of these other stocks of carbon vary from year to year, even by just a few percentage points, they would override human influence on the atmosphere.

A scientific understanding of the global distribution of carbon is evidently needed but matters are far from straightforward. For one thing the facts cited in the last paragraph are far from indisputable. Estimations of the amount of carbon in the plants of a rain forest or in African soils are just that – estimations. So too are the stated amounts of carbon in the world's oceans. These facts are conjectural in just the way I described earlier in this chapter when I discussed the nature of botanists' knowledge. And when these facts are put to use – even to quite simple use – some of the difficulties become apparent. When scientists do the sums to work out where all the humanly-emitted carbon dioxide goes, the totals do not add up (Pearce 1989, p. 115). Carbon levels in the atmosphere do not appear to be increasing as quickly as carbon dioxide is being discharged into it. Consequently, carbon must somewhere be being withdrawn from the air. Given the destruction of the tropical rain forests, the loss of high quality soil and the death or clearance of forests in more temperate areas, it seems very unlikely that plant life and soils can be soaking it up. Yet ocean scientists do not accept that the seas are able to extract the gas from the atmosphere at the rate which would be necessary to account for the missing carbon.

It is surprisingly difficult just to do the carbon 'budgets'. It is all the more difficult to understand how the world's stores of carbon will respond to the greenhouse effect – will the natural stores of carbon tend to absorb the atmospheric surplus or will global warming lead carbon dioxide to be released from the reserves and thus exacerbate the problem? It turns out that some very complex and unexpected areas of science have something to say on this matter.

In Chapter 1, when I introduced the greenhouse effect, I described how the earth's temperature was kept reasonably constant by the regulation of carbon dioxide. Plants absorb carbon dioxide and produce oxygen; most other forms of life consume oxygen. This might lead one to anticipate that the earth's temperature has tended to remain stable. In comparison with other planets this is probably so. But from the point of view of terrestrial animals the story looks rather different. To them, the earth's history would seem to have been characterized by large temperature variations, including periods of extreme cold in the ice ages. Studies of the causes of ice ages have suggested mechanisms which may govern or at least influence the globe's temperature control. One factor believed to be a basic cause of changes in global climate is beyond any imaginable human control: the earth's orbit around the sun, which is not completely consistent. In effect the earth wobbles on its axis in a variety of ways, slightly changing its orientation to the sun a few times every 100,000 years. During some parts of this slow wobble the poles receive less heat than usual. They would therefore be expected to cool, allowing ice to build up. As the polar ice sheets expand they reflect more of the sun's heat back into space, thus intensifying the cooling. The growth of ice might become self-sustaining, at least until the earth's position shifts and warming is recommenced.

If this was the whole story, ice ages would have little to teach us about the greenhouse effect. However, as Pearce explains (1989, pp. 139–56), the oceans may contribute to the onset and to the ending of ice ages through their influence over atmospheric carbon dioxide. This may occur in either of two ways. First, the oceans may have a direct physical influence on this greenhouse gas. On top of all the daily and seasonal currents in the oceans, driven by the wind and the tides, there is one major pattern of oceanic flow: comparatively warm water flows on the surface of the oceans from the north Pacific, past Indonesia, and southern Africa and up into the north Atlantic.[5] Between Norway and Greenland, where the warm flow (known in the north Atlantic as the Gulf Stream) meets the cold of the Arctic, the water cools and dives to commence the return flow, past the Antarctic to the Pacific. The amount of water involved is vast, as is its effect on the atmosphere: 'In the far north Atlantic, twenty million cubic metres of water descend to the bottom of the ocean every second . . . The north Atlantic may swallow up several billion tonnes of carbon dioxide each year in this way' (Pearce 1989, pp. 140–1). During ice ages, when water is locked up in ice sheets and thus withheld from the oceans, the operation of this global current may be affected. To take an exaggeratedly simple example, a halt in its flow during ice ages could lead less carbon dioxide to be absorbed by the oceans. The gas would then accumulate in the atmosphere, the greenhouse effect would begin to set in and the earth would gradually warm up, hastening the end of the ice age. By the same token, if present-day global warming comes to heat the oceans, this too might impede the oceanic circulation since it could reduce the temperature differences which drive the circulating currents. In the long run, this might well compound our greenhouse problems.

The second anticipated influence on the greenhouse effect is a biological one. Ice ages would clearly have a decisive impact on marine and terrestrial life. It is easy to imagine how biological and climatical factors could interact. Again to take a simple example, if the cold began to kill off the plants and animals in the sea which absorb carbon dioxide (for photosynthesis and for building up their shells respectively), the greenhouse effect would begin. Then, as the temperatures began to rise, life would proliferate and the greenhouse gas would be withdrawn from the atmosphere. However, it seems that the interaction was far more complex than this (Pearce 1989, pp. 143–50). At first, the arrival of ice ages was probably accelerated by biological factors. Perhaps falling sea-levels laid bare more land which could be eroded; perhaps water was locked up in the form of ice, leaving the continents dry and leading to an increase in the amount of dust. Either way, more nutrients (like iron and nitrogen) reached the seas and biological productivity rose accordingly. This withdrew carbon dioxide from the air and led to an anti-greenhouse effect, cooling the earth further. Gradually, though, the nutrient supply from land would have begun to become exhausted. To some extent the nutrients could be recycled in the surface layers of the seas but slowly they would have been lost to the deep ocean. Marine life would then have rapidly diminished and its cooling contribution ceased. This interpretation of events might well have practical implications for our reaction to today's greenhouse problem. For example, if nutrients radically affect the ocean's uptake of carbon dioxide, it might be possible to treat the ocean with chemicals to promote marine life, and this should lead to reductions in global warming (Pearce 1989, p. 151).

These brief comments on recent attempts to understand the workings of the oceans and atmosphere can only give a flavour of the scientific complexities involved. They will, though, serve to bear out the claims that I made earlier.

The greenhouse effect cannot be understood and responded to without scientific expertise. But a scientifically authoritative interpretation of the greenhouse effect is still far from us; in some respects, we even seem to become less certain the more we study it. Knowledge about the oceans is hard to come by. We cannot observe the deep ocean current in any straightforward sense. In the 1990s scientists hope to begin this observation by tracking water movements through the satellite monitoring of buoys and the sonic detection of weighted 'drifters' moving with oceanic currents (Williams, 1990a). In addition to problems of observation, the 'science of the greenhouse' is hindered by theoretical uncertainty and by the problems posed by an open environment. We have seen the conflicting theoretical interpretations of the causes of ice ages; such disagreements abound in studies of the greenhouse effect. Additionally, the climate and the oceans are amongst the most open and complicated systems which scientists have tried to model.

Before concluding this section I should make clear that these observations are not intended as criticisms of science nor as a denial of the importance of global warming. I know of no one who argues that we should continue blithely to discharge carbon dioxide from our motor vehicles and power stations. For one thing, by using our fuel resources more sparingly we reduce all manner of pollution apart from carbon dioxide, as well as lowering energy costs. But my interest in this chapter is in the role played by scientific authority. Science is needed to offer authoritative advice on our environmental problems but – for understandable, yet persistent reasons – that authority is not as decisive as environmentalists might desire. Indeed, environmentalists find themselves in a situation that is hardly different from that faced by other groups making social problem claims. Despite the fact that they look to scientific authority to support their views, environmentalists must still endure claims and counter-claims – for example that nuclear power is hazardous or that it offers the solution to global warming. Science does not underwrite their social problem claims in any straightforward way. Accordingly, science is not the good, unwavering friend that many environmentalists would like it to be.

SCIENCE AS AN UNRELIABLE
FRIEND – EPISTEMOLOGICALLY

Up to this point we have examined ways in which *in fact* science may be less good as an ally than conservationists anticipate. It may not provide the answers on occasions when it would be politic to have them; it may leave the public impatient of factlessness; and some of the facts which conservationists would like to marshall may be elusive. But in some cases these deficiencies come close to endemic problems of scientific knowledge – to do with science as a way of knowing at all. Most nature conservationists would defend science as a form of knowledge by pointing to its observational basis and its methodic development. But, as we have seen and as Nicholson makes clear, the observational basis is open to discrepant interpretations. As soon as there arise competing and plausible accounts of what the observed facts are, then the basis that appears so secure becomes itself problematic. The empirical and provisional basis of scientific knowledge – its apparent strength – can readily be re-formulated as an *uncertain* basis.

This argument achieves its most spectacular form when it is posed as the philosophical problem of 'induction'. For centuries philosophers have pointed out that although, for example, we may believe that the sun will rise tomorrow because it has risen every day so far, this can only be an assumption. We cannot know such things for certain. In the past, traditionalists tended to use such arguments to contrast science unfavourably with other paradigms of knowledge, such as religion or logic. Logical deduction appears more certain than empirical induction.

In recent years these arguments have not been regarded as having much practical importance. People have not worried about the likelihood of there being a sunrise tomorrow. But this line of thought does show up the Achilles heel of science, a weakness which can be used in a practical way to evade scientific authority. Those opposed to a scientific judgement can always say that science is not fully certain and that, for this reason, they do not recognize expert scientific opinion as ultimately authoritative.

As one might expect, environmentalists tend to play down this issue in many public contexts. Thus, in a recent issue of the *BBC Wildlife Magazine*, Jonathon Porritt wrote (1989, p. 353),

> the scientists are now with us rather than against us. On occasions . . . they actually seem to be out in front of the activists of the Environment Movement. In the early seventies, the protagonists of the 'limits to growth' scenario relied primarily on an inadequately programmed computer model. Politicians had little difficulty dismissing it as sensationalist speculation. Today, there's nothing speculative about the depletion of the ozone layer, the deforestation of the Amazon, the build-up of carbon dioxide in the atmosphere, or the pesticide residues in our water and food. Hard scientific evidence counts for a lot in a hard materialistic world.

It is interesting to note that scientific proof is associated with hard materialism, almost as though scientific support for environmental policies would not be needed in a more compassionate society. None the less, this embrace of the 'hardness' of scientific evidence displays the kind of strategy that can be adopted in chasing off the horrors of doubt.

Similarly, to take another recent example, in 1989 Greenpeace ran a newspaper advertisement campaign in the UK opposing claims by the then Environment Minister, Nicholas Ridley, that increased investment in nuclear power generation would help solve the greenhouse problem. The minister was pictured with his pro-nuclear assertion printed across his mouth; beneath it was written: 'scientifically speaking, it's just a lot of hot air' (see for example *The Independent* 5 July 1989, p. 9). Greenpeace then printed a declaration disagreeing with Mr Ridley, a declaration apparently signed by '100 of the country's leading scientists, doctors, and engineers'. Now, there is something curious about the logic of this move for although Greenpeace is invoking scientific authority, it also seems to be claiming that it enjoys the support of the *majority* of scientists. Its argument seems to be not just that 'scientific opinion' is with Greenpeace, but that *a lot of* scientists think this way. Yet, one could just as easily argue that in the context of the UK, one hundred 'scientists, doctors and engineers' is actually very few. I suggest that Greenpeace was forced into this roundabout appeal because it was confronted by an interpretative difficulty. It wished to claim to be in the right epistemologically – to say that Mr Ridley was simply wrong. Yet, while the epistemological right may in principle be straightforward and unambiguous, in practice both sides in any dispute can usually count on some scientific supporters. Both sides may try to claim the epistemological high ground. An appeal to large numbers of qualified supporters is perhaps the simplest way to respond to this difficulty in a mass public medium.

Whatever the complexities of enlisting scientific authority in a positive fashion, from the conservationists' point of view the difficulty is most acutely felt when it goes the other way – when they are confronted with the barrier of scientific proof. As Richard North, *The Independent*'s environment correspondent, has noted (1987, p. 15):[6] 'Even now, scientific exactitude can debilitate conservation by insisting (as governments rejoice to notice) that the evidence of damage caused must be total: which it almost never will be.' This argumentative strategy is probably best known in the UK through its use in relation to acid rain. As we saw in Chapters 1 and 3, the authorities used the lack of certain knowledge that acid rain (and in particular British acid rain) was responsible for the death of trees and the acidification of lakes in Europe as a justification for continuing with power station emissions.

Different groups adopt a different kind of response to this problem. Greenpeace, whom North was criticizing in his article in *The Independent*, tends to be impatient of the limitations of scientific proof. North accepts that Greenpeace may be correct to suppose that it 'would get little [media] coverage were it to stick to the facts. In any case, it does not' (1987, p. 15). He goes on to list ways in which Greenpeace's public statements have been, as he puts it, 'economical with the truth'. His contention seems to be that Greenpeace has often bent the scientific truth to make issues appear more grave than they truly are in order to stir people into action. This bending has, for example, taken the form of over-generalizing from atypical examples. It remains unclear what strategy North would endorse, given the uncertainties which inevitably accompany 'good' scientific practice. Moreover, it should be appreciated that activist organizations can point to a number of occasions on which their gloomy expectations have been vindicated – when further spills or leaks have followed assurances that the 'problem' has been overcome. With some plausibility they could argue that there is a practical asymmetry between doing nothing (the situation will worsen) and doing something (it may bring unnecessary cost but no permanent damage to the environment). Other organizations adopt a self-consciously contrasting tone. For example, the chairman of the Ulster Wildlife Trust recently characterized his group as standing for 'informed, educated, reasonable, rational conservation'. This seems to advocate a different epistemological stance from that adopted by Greenpeace but the problem, of course, is how to confront urgent but uncertain issues rationally and reasonably.

The specific epistemological character of science thus leads to difficulties when groups try to 'cash in' on scientific authority. If you are relentlessly committed to scientific proprieties, you will not be able to make instant, unequivocal judgements. But if you are not publicly committed in this way, you are open to criticism. The resulting practical difficulties may become apparent during scientific disputes or in public controversies. But they can also surface in a virulent form in specialized forums of debate. In particular, the conventions of legal cross-examination and the standards of legal proof may not mesh well with the character of scientific argument and expertise.

CASE STUDY: LEGAL INTERPRETATIONS OF SCIENTIFIC CERTAINTY

A number of case studies have shown that scientific arguments often do not stand up in court or in public inquiries as well as might be expected from the general public authority enjoyed by science (see the studies in Smith and Wynne 1988 as well as Oteri, Weinberg and Pinales 1982; Wynne 1982; Yearley 1989). In part this may be explained by circumstantial factors. After all, the majority of scientists are unaccustomed to the kind of questioning to which they are subjected in court. Further, skilled examiners can use the fact that the discussion is not free – that the questioner has great control over the topic – to weaken the scientists' presentation. But scientists also fare badly because legal procedure can focus on apparent weaknesses in science as a form of knowledge.

To illustrate this point we can turn to the case of a public inquiry into plans to develop a Northern Irish peat bog for horticultural peat extraction (Yearley 1989). In the late 1980s government ecologists had conducted a survey and evaluation of Northern Irish bogs, held to be an increasingly endangered habitat. But a peat-cutting company had already taken steps to develop one of the bogs that had come out as highly rated in this survey. A public inquiry was called to determine whether development should be allowed to proceed. The developers were represented by a senior barrister while the conservationists relied on scientifically trained representatives. Although the barrister might have been expected to try to circumvent the witnesses' scientific skills (for example, by concentrating on the trade-off between economic development and conservation or by highlighting details of legal procedure), he chose to confront the scientific witnesses directly. In doing so he called attention to important characteristics of scientific expertise.

In essence the barrister adopted two lines of argument. First, he questioned the scoring system by means of which the surveyed bogs had been assessed. For example, bogs may be valued because they are virtually intact or because they are home to a wide variety of plant species. To some extent the rankings of the various bogs in the survey depended on how these, and other, attributes were weighted. The barrister thus suggested that the scores were merely a convention and could, in fact, have been very different. In effect the scores were just a construct, an artefact. Yet, he claimed, the scientists 'behaved as though the scores were "written on tablets of stone"' (Yearley 1989, p. 431). The scientists could not show for certain that the technique adopted was the best way of scoring bogs; therefore, it could be implied, their scoring system was of little worth.

It is important to note an asymmetry here (see Oteri, Weinberg and Pinales 1982, p. 258). The barrister did not have to demonstrate that there was a good scoring system according to which the bog in question could safely be developed. He only had to cast doubt on the scoring system that had been used in this case. The developer's argument traded on the scientists' lack

of absolute authority, in other words on the epistemological
character of science.

His second argument operated to similar effect. Not every
feature of a bog that might be important to conservation could
be represented in the scoring system. For example, in the case
of the disputed bog, there were two striking additional features,
one favouring the bog, the other compromising its likely value.
On the one hand it supported a rare butterfly but, on the other,
its shape was elongated rather than circular and thus unusually
prone to drying out. Neither of these features was represented
in the scoring system yet both were alluded to by witnesses.
The legal representative was able to use this fact to argue that
the assessment of the bog was actually *ad hoc* rather than
methodic. As we saw earlier in this chapter, scientific expertise
must depend on elements of judgement and on craft skill. These
informal aspects of science can be highlighted to make scientific
evidence appear like mere opinion.

There is one further way in which the limitations of science
as a form of authority or as a way of knowing may surface
as a practical weakness. This too can be illustrated using data
from a public inquiry. As described in Chapter 3, some environmental groups are hoping to benefit from the 'conservation
business' by, for example, acting as consultants. Money raised
in this way reduces their dependence on government grants
and should, therefore, enhance their freedom of action. Their
scientific expertise is very important in this regard.

Some of the implications of this practice were highlighted
when a public inquiry was recently called in Northern Ireland
to examine rival plans to build a yachting marina in an area
of importance for wildlife conservation. One of the competing
developers had contracted the UWT's consultancy service to
undertake a preliminary environmental impact assessment of
their proposed development. However, in addition to accepting
this contract, the trust appeared at the inquiry as a pressure
group, objecting in various ways to aspects of each of the
developers' schemes. Staff of the trust were dismayed when the
inquiry's commissioner refused the UWT permission to offer
criticisms of the proposal for which they had performed the
study. The view of the scientists in the trust was that they
had carried out an objective survey for the developers and

that they had as much right as any other group to lodge an objection to that developer's plans. But in the eyes of the commissioner at the inquiry this would be to have 'two bites at the cherry'. He ruled that it was not possible to separate their factual findings from their opinions in this way. Equally, there was a danger that the legal representatives of the other developers could suggest that the trust had been more lenient towards its former paymaster than to the other developers. The impartiality of scientific testimony, to which the trust's representatives were straightforwardly committed, can readily be called into question. Thus, powerful though scientific authority may be, in legal and commercial contexts it may exhibit specific practical weaknesses.

SCIENCE AS AN INSUFFICIENT FRIEND

The green movement's dependence on science may not bring it the cognitive authority it seeks either in practice or principle. But there are some environmental arguments where its insufficiency seems to be of another sort. Take the case of the Marine Conservation Society's concern for the basking shark. It says that this shark is an animal that does no harm to humans and that is majestic in its own way. Sadly, our fishing practices endanger it and we should protect it for its own sake. At present, relatively little is known about these creatures, so the lack of empirical information is a handicap to the campaign. But, let us suppose that we did know all about these sharks and that they are actually in danger. It might still be possible to argue that the sharks are not worth the loss of fishing. What this suggests is that the arguments for the green case are far from solely scientific; indeed they look rather similar to those surrounding abortion and artistic freedom.

As I stated in the Introduction, this book is not a moral analysis. It is not my intention to argue about whether conservation is morally worthy (for a review of ecologism as a philosophy see Dobson 1990). What is important at this point is to note that the scientific correctness of the greens' analysis – even when that correctness is undisputed – still does not carry many clear implications for practical action. If it is believed that the destruction of the ozone layer will result in many human deaths then possibly there is a common practical need to take steps to remedy the problem. But in the case of the majority of other environmental problems the practical implications are more disputable. We saw in Chapter 1 the variety of reasons offered for saving the rain forests: for the sake of the tribespeople who live there, for the sake of the plants and animals themselves, on account of the likely medicinal value of rain forest plants and so on. The same variety was encountered in the discussion of arguments for species conservation. There is much room for negotiation about the exact practical imperatives that follow from such arguments.

Environmentalists tend to invoke as many of these reasons as they can in order to attract the greatest number of supporters. As we have seen, people may join a group or give money for a wide variety of reasons. The RSPB appeals to naturalists, to bird enthusiasts and to those with a diffuse concern for the countryside. Greenpeace attracts animal lovers as well as those opposed to the nuclear industry. Those who become committed to working for groups making social problem claims in the environmental area tend to adopt the organization's objectives as their own personal aims. For this reason, the exact moral basis of the groups, even of the movement as a whole, seldom needs to be explored.

Thus, although science is used in making social problem claims, science itself does not dictate which claims will be made. For instance, the RSPB draws on considerable scientific skills in conserving birds but it was not scientific reasons that led the group to work for birds rather than field mice and voles. Science is not a sufficient guide to what conservation groups should concentrate on and prioritize; nor, often, does science provide the members' reasons for engaging in conservation activities. In a narrow sense, science does not seem to compel people to conserve particular bits of their environment nor tell them what the conservation priorities are.

RE-MORALIZING SCIENCE: GAIA

Up to this point I have suggested that science seems not to offer a moral basis for the green case. However, the 1980s witnessed a great growth in popularity for an idea which ties the science of the environment to moral concern for the planet: the Gaia hypothesis. This hypothesis can best be explained through an example. Earlier on, during my discussion of the science of the greenhouse effect, I described how the amount of carbon dioxide in the atmosphere seems to have *regulated* the earth's temperature. To talk in this way about 'regulation' might seem suspect and anthropomorphic. After all, there was no one there to do the regulating. However, most people are happy to talk in this way, regarding the description as a metaphor.

But the Gaia hypothesis proposes that it is not just a metaphor; according to it, the earth really is regulated. Life on the planet is somehow co-ordinated in a way that works to keep the planet habitable. On this view, the planet should properly be regarded as a superorganism. Jim Lovelock, who proposed this idea, gave the name Gaia (the earth goddess) to the workings of this superorganism. Clearly, if the earth can be thought of in this way it might change our expectations of the globe's response to human meddling and alter our attitude to the planet – we might now see ourselves as having a moral obligation not just to humans and animals but to Gaia.

Supporters of the Gaian idea would claim that it has helped them understand the ecology of the earth through its emphasis on the contribution which living organisms make to the maintenance of the world. Gaian ideas stress the extent to which the planet is suffused with life. Surprisingly few physical processes operate without the intervention of living organisms. For example, we have already seen how organisms in the sea may play a central role in determining the earth's temperature by controlling the amount of carbon dioxide in the atmosphere. Similarly, soils are not simple, inorganic materials. Organisms which live in soils are essential to their biological productivity. Thus, a demythologized Gaia hypothesis might amount to a belief amongst scientists that living things are empirically more important to the physics and chemistry of the earth than has hitherto been recognized.

However, this demythologized version is not the only one in circulation. More overtly holistic Gaian ideas have proved attractive to some scientists and to many in the environmental movement (see Porritt and Winner 1988, pp. 249–53). At the same time other scientists have perceived these ideas as deeply disturbing. Sceptical scientists raise both empirical and logical doubts.

At an empirical level, for example, one might seek to query the hypothesis by citing the contribution which organisms appear to have made to the intensification of global cooling at the start of ice ages. Surely, it might be said, Gaia would counteract rather than assist such cooling? But most arguments have been addressed to the logic of the Gaia hypothesis. Thus it is argued that there are problems about the idea of ascribing purposes to Gaia. If it is to be more than a metaphor, Gaia would seem to need to have purposes in the way that only humans and (conceivably) a few animals do. Scientists do not treat plants or bacteria as though they had deliberate intentions; how then can the planet possess them? Even, sceptics argue, if one accepts that it might be possible to talk of the planet's purpose, it is impossible to know what that purpose is. We cannot communicate with the planet. As Horsfall asks, 'what is her purpose – to perpetuate the rock endoskeleton, to ensure the safety of the majority of species, to ensure the safety of certain key elements such as bacteria, or to ensure the safety of Men?' (1990). From time to time, as we have seen, there are ice ages and other catastrophies which result in mass fatalities. How can these be reconciled with Gaia's assumed purposes? Of course, one could say that the purpose is not to retain any particular life form but an aggregate life force but, since we do not know how to count this aggregate, we could never test such a theory.

Many scientists felt indignant about Lovelock's claims; for several years his papers were routinely turned down by leading journals (Pearce 1989, p. 37). In a recent denunciation in the *Guardian* Horsfall dismisses Lovelock as a 'scientist of sorts' and claims that his ideas appeal only to 'scientifically illiterate greens' (1990). As with morals, it is not my role to try to decide which view is scientifically correct. The pragmatic strength of the Gaia hypothesis is that it offers to combine environmental science with morality. It thus seems to provide the kind of authority which, as we have seen, a more routine dependence on science fails to deliver. Horsfall fears that this easy authority may incline greens to authoritarianism. Gaia certainly has the potential to offer a form of transcendent certainty but, as mentioned in Chapter 3, there are strong tendencies within the green movement which render totalitarianism unlikely. Within the context of the environmental movement, attacks such as that by Horsfall may backfire on scientists who feel that their leading role is slipping away from ecologists and natural historians into the hands of ideologues. They may lose some of the authority and popularity in the movement which they currently enjoy.

CONCLUSION

In Chapter 2 we saw that environmental organizations can be understood as engaged in the making of social problem claims. At first sight the fact that they can call on scientific support in making these claims might appear to give them a decisive advantage over other types of pressure group. Science can be a friend to the environmental movement but we can now see that it is a less comprehensively powerful friend than might be supposed. Scientific authority has specific weaknesses; its authority is also insufficiently broad to supply a complete underpinning for the green case. Environmentalism needs the support it draws from science but that support is not sufficient to grant it public authority and political success. Accordingly, the future of the green case will be shaped by factors other than the correctness of environmentalists' claims. One of the most important of these other factors is the response to environmental issues by the governments and peoples of the Third World, who, after all, comprise the majority of the world's citizens. It is to this subject that we turn in the next chapter.

NOTES

1 The research from which the data used in this chapter derive was supported by the UK ESRC, grant A0925 0006, under the programme on the Public Understanding of Science. The study, using interview and participant observation, ran from 1987 to 1989.

2 As mentioned in Chapter 2 the Ulster Wildlife Trust is effectively the county trust for Northern Ireland and is affiliated to the RSNC.

3 After the period of fieldwork for my research TBT (tributyl tin) was withdrawn from use.

4   As described in Chapter 2, the RSPB is increasingly interested in the places
    to which British birds migrate and in preserving crucial sites along migration
    routes. For this, scientific tracking is needed.

    The issue of multi-caused fatalities was recently illustrated by the case of
    racing pigeons which, apparently, suffer high rates of attrition, particularly
    on popular cross-Channel races. This was blamed by many on peregrines
    which, although protected by law, were therefore being shot by fanciers
    and, in one spectacular instance, even killed by 'kamikaze' pigeons (ageing
    birds fitted with explosive charges).

5   This is to simplify an already simplified account. The pattern of flow is
    rather more complicated than I suggest here, see Pearce 1989, pp. 139–43.
    In particular, some of the deep-water current rises in the Antarctic.

6   North also addressed this argument in his Radio 4 programme about
    Greenpeace broadcast on 6 December 1989 and entitled 'The Zero
    Option'.

CHAPTER 5

Development and the environment

INTRODUCTION: DEVELOPMENT OR DEPENDENCY?

Up to this point we have focused largely on the growth of environmental politics and the green movement in the developed world. Certainly, much of the advance in green awareness has taken place in the most highly developed regions of the globe, often referred to as the 'north' (defined to include Australasia). But we should not overlook the fact that there are Green Parties in, for example, Mongolia and Brazil (*Guardian* 27 April 1990, p. 27 and Parkin 1989, pp. 314–15 respectively) as well as groups affiliated to Friends of the Earth International in Brazil, Argentina and Pakistan. Even if the growth of the movement has been greatest in the north, as we saw in the first chapter, many environmental problems are at their most severe in the Third World (or the 'south'). It is there that the rain forests are being cut down, there that toxic wastes are illegally dumped, there that the most endangered species live and there that desertification threatens agriculture.

To some extent it is an accident of geography that these problems are concentrated in this way. But many social scientists would argue that there are more systematic forces at work too. They would argue that the countries of the developing world have many common social, political and economic features which make them susceptible to environmental problems. In turn, it is suggested that these countries' common features should be understood within a unified social scientific framework. The central notions in this framework are those of underdevelopment and dependency.

Until after the Second World War much of the Third World was divided up between the northern – primarily European – powers or was closely linked to the dominant economies, such as the USA and Britain. There were few states seeking to develop in an autonomous way. It was only as the number of independent countries grew that policy makers and analysts began to ask how nations could emulate the success of the north. Initial social scientific studies of the emerging Third World assumed that these countries were more or less in the condition that had characterized Europe prior to its industrialization. On this assumption, it was reasonable to expect that they could be analysed using the concepts devised for the study of the transformation of Europe. Perhaps development demanded a change from cultures characterized, in Durkheim's famous terms, by mechanical solidarity to societies based on organic solidarity. Or maybe what was required was the emergence of a cultural change akin to that Weber had described in *The Protestant Ethic and the Spirit of Capitalism* (1904). The apparent failure of many Third-World countries to develop as quickly or successfully as had been hoped was attributed to obstacles to their modernization, whether cultural, economic, or political. If only they would become more modern, it was suggested, they would develop successfully. The deficiency was largely laid at these countries' own doors.

However, an opposing tradition of analysis emerged which was more or less typified by a view of the Third World as the subject of systematic exploitation. Analyses in this tradition suggested that the Third World could not be equated with the First World at an earlier stage of its development. In support of this view, social scientists pointed out that Third-World nations had to compete with technically sophisticated industry coming from the enormously wealthy countries of the north. At the opposite extreme, early industrial England had had virtually no competitors during its development, certainly none which were technically more advanced. The analogy between early modern Europe and the present-day south just does not hold.

On top of this, it was argued that a history of economic exploitation had to be taken into account. The First World had succeeded by preying on its colonies, using them as sources of raw materials and labour and as manipulable markets in which to sell its goods. By contrast, the nations of the Third World had suffered from this exploitation. And, for that matter, they now had no one to exploit. Authors writing in this tradition argued for a strong contrast between the north and the south. Early on, the First World had lacked development; it had been simply *un*developed. But the modern Third World was not undeveloped. Its position was in many respects worse and could best be described as *under*developed (see Harrison 1988, pp. 62–99).

THE SOCIAL CORRELATES OF DEPENDENCY

We can begin to examine the societal consequences of under-development by taking agricultural production as an illustrative example. Advocates of this analytic approach argue that Third-World agriculture is not simply in a poor state of development as perhaps had been the case in early modern Europe. Agriculture in the south has been actively underdeveloped: in many cases the best land was taken over for the production of crops which were required by the factories or the markets of the imperial powers. Cultivation in the colonies was organized for the benefit of the colonizer rather than to meet the needs of local people. One consequence of this arrangement is that the agricultural production of the Third World only makes sense in relation to the economic needs of the north. Only metropolitan demand for sugar and tea, for example, could justify the plantation economy. In this sense, the south is dependent on the north. While they were still colonies, the southern lands were literally dependent. They were generally administered to suit imperial needs. However, analysts of the Third World would argue that this dependency has persisted after the ending of formal colonial status. Southern agriculturalists are still dependent on demand from the rich countries, and they rely on the north for processing and shipping. Commonly, even the price of their produce is established in the commodity markets of the north's financial centres. Using evidence of this sort, social scientists have claimed that underdevelopment is associated with economic and political dependency. Dependency theorists contend that 'development' in the Third World has failed to result in autonomous political growth and economic independence. Steps taken to 'develop' too often lead to more dependency.

Although I have illustrated this theoretical perspective with the example of agriculture, it applies to other areas also. Many Third-World countries are highly dependent on the export of minerals; their national income may even rest essentially on a single commodity. Thus, at the start of the 1980s Jamaica was 78 per cent dependent on bauxite (aluminium ore) for its export income, while Niger relied on uranium ore for 83 per cent of its income and Zambia received 87 per cent of its earnings from copper (Kidron and Segal 1984, p. 19).[1] The exporting countries have very little control over the prices fetched by these commodities. The price is effectively set by demand in the industries of the First World and by the markets in the trading centres such as London and Tokyo. To take an example, Bolivia is famously dependent on tin mining which, in the early 1980s, accounted for around one third of its export income. (It is also a major exporter of another metal, antimony.) But then worldwide use of tin declined strongly. Because of the way the markets responded to this decline, 'Tin prices collapsed by over 80 per cent in 1985 and never recovered. Bolivian inflation that same year attained a mind-boggling 25,000 per cent' (George 1988, p. 149). By the end of the following year, 70 per cent of employees of the state-owned Comibol mining company in Bolivia had lost their jobs (Hayter 1989, p. 153). The country's export earnings slumped disastrously and the sudden growth in unemployment meant that there was much less money for domestic spending. Events which were almost wholly beyond Bolivian control caused massive disruption to the economy and social structure. Bolivia's economic dependence can be very plainly seen.

Dependency is experienced in relation to manufacture also. Lacking capital, underdeveloped countries have generally been keen to attract industrial investment. When it comes to negotiating the terms for these investments their bargaining position is characteristically weak. They may offer financial inducements to bring investors to their country, such as assistance with building costs or a period of exemption from taxes. The idea is that, once wooed into the country, the company will stay. But if the initial terms are very favourable it is possible for companies to recover their costs quickly and then move on to another host. Alternatively, they may use the threat of withdrawal to re-negotiate terms, thus winning further concessions from the host government. Attempts to attract foreign investment can thus reinforce economic dependence and compromise the nation's control over its industrial and trade policies. The likelihood of this outcome is increased by the fact that much investment in the Third World has been carried out by very large, powerful overseas companies usually referred to as transnational corporations (TNCs). In many cases these companies are every bit as wealthy as the countries with which they are dealing; for example, in the mid-1980s General Motors had annual sales worth more in dollars than the gross domestic product of nearly every individual Latin American country (Jenkins, 1987, p. 9).[2] For its part, IBM was wealthier than the Philippines while du Pont's product was almost exactly comparable to that of the whole of Pakistan. Given these economic conditions, it is unlikely that states will have the upper hand in negotiations over investment.

Dealings with advanced foreign companies can also result in the problems associated with 'technological dependence' (Stewart 1978, pp. 114–40; Yearley 1988, pp. 146–55). Technologies devised in the countries of the First World tend to be designed to be labour saving, capital intensive and technically complex. These features threaten to make the technology inappropriate for the Third World. When these technologies are introduced into an underdeveloped country their high cost is a drain on the nation's wealth. At the same time, few jobs are created since the equipment was designed to economize on labour, bearing in mind the high wage costs in the First World. So, when the underdeveloped world gets access to the best, latest technology, poor countries with a labour surplus receive expensive, labour-saving machinery.

Within the Third World these arrangements serve to reinforce divisions between the poor majority, who use traditional low-productivity technologies, and the wealthier, modernized minority. The complexity of the technology dictates that it must often be serviced or repaired by engineers from the developed world. Moreover, the research and development facilities of large

international companies are typically retained in the north so
that the nations of the south have to look to the developed
world for new instalments of technology. Finally, according
to Hoogvelt, companies in the north may use the technical
specificity of their equipment as a way of retaining control
over Third-World enterprises:

> By making the physical characteristics of their plant and
> machinery, of their technical operation, and of their end-
> product, critically different from other similar machinery,
> processes and products that are available in the world mar-
> kets, [these companies] can establish and preserve future
> supply, servicing and maintenance links quite independently
> of any written agreement or any form of legal ownership.
> (Hoogvelt 1982, p. 69)

Technological dependency is likely to arise whenever Third-
World countries receive technically advanced manufacturing
equipment from the north. In some cases, though, it seems
that this form of dependency is encouraged by TNCs as a way
of safeguarding their economic interest.

So far we have looked at the meaning of dependency in terms
of overtly economic activities; it has been used to make sense
of the lack of economic success in the south despite the mineral
and agricultural endowments of many countries and years of
investment from the north. But it also describes a cultural
relationship. For example, scientific research in Third-World
universities tends to look to the metropolitan 'core' where most
of the leading work is done and where the principal scientific
journals are edited. In most respects, the core sets the agenda
for science (Yearley 1988, pp. 156–8). The same is true for
broadcast media, particularly given the north's dominance in
satellite technology. The dependent relationship is evident in
'high' culture and even, despite the recent vogue for 'world
music', in popular culture.

The descriptive and empirical value of analyses in terms of
dependency is widely recognized but the theoretical value of
the term is disputed. For one thing, some countries seem to
have been more successful at escaping dependency than others.
South Korea and Taiwan have both been heavily dependent on

the USA for economic aid and political sponsorship. Yet they have recorded great economic advances; they make a profit on their international trade and, in the last decade, have begun to sell large quantities of technically advanced consumer goods to the First World. Furthermore, as Berger (1987) argues, it would be difficult not to classify Japan as having been a dependent nation. Its economy was forced open to international trade in the middle of the nineteenth century, then it was invaded – not to say devastated – by the USA in 1945, and its culture has since been deeply influenced by Western tastes. But in the last thirty years its development has been spectacular.

Berger is strongly critical of dependency theory, arguing that it is undermined by its inability to account for the rise of Japan and the other economic successes of East Asia. He takes a rather cynical view of its appeal:

Its statist bias directly serves the vested interests of political elites. Beyond those vested interests, however, it serves a very useful psychological function. If the roots of underdevelopment are to be sought *outside* one's own society, one is spared often painful (and personally embarrassing) self-examination and one is provided with very convenient external scapegoats. This [explains] the popularity of this viewpoint in the Third World. (1987, p. 128, original emphasis)

Certainly, subscribers to dependency theory do claim to find an explanation for the misfortunes of Third-World countries beyond their borders and may be led to overlook the (sometimes woeful) policies adopted by Third-World governments. They are also led to look away from the cultural and religious differences between the societies of the south, and simply to class them all as underdeveloped.

The theory also suffers from certain ambiguities (see Harrison 1988, pp. 110–20). Thus, in many respects Canada has the appearance of dependency. It exports many primary materials, particularly timber products, to the USA and its economy is strongly influenced by trends in its neighbour's financial well-being. Yet few people would characterize Canada as a typical dependent country. One suspects that Third-World citizens would happily settle for dependency if it resulted in a Canadian standard of living in a Canadian democracy. Equally, advocates of the theory, keen to emphasize the distinctiveness of the underdeveloped world's experience, may overlook similar episodes in the West's own history. While land use in the underdeveloped world was often geared towards the satisfaction of colonial needs, land use in the core countries was directed to serving the needs of the elite. It is not clear that the economic exploitation suffered in the Third World is of a qualitatively different kind from that endured in, say, Cornwall or northern Scotland. That is not to deny that these areas suffered deprivation. Rather it is to acknowledge that the spread of capitalist wealth ultimately acted to reduce their deprivation. If that can happen during the industrialization of the West, why can it not occur in the Third World?

Finally, the cases of those countries which do seem to be industrializing successfully under capitalism (Taiwan, Hong Kong, South Korea and so on) suggest that, at least in some instances, market mechanisms may actually favour developing nations. Since their wage rates tend to be lower, they have a natural price advantage in some stages of manufacture. They can use this advantage to attract investment and gradually develop their own skills and expertise in manufacture.

For present purposes we do not need to come to a resolution of this debate. We can accept dependency as an empirical generalization applying to many Third-World countries, a generalization which even Berger is willing to accept (1987, p. 122). We can also note that such successes as Taiwan are still in the minority when compared to the countries of South and Central America, the Caribbean, Africa and South Asia. We do not need to worry which is the exception and which is the rule – whether the peculiar thing is that some countries, like Taiwan, have escaped the economic malaise of the south or whether it is the peristent poverty of nations such as Bolivia which needs a special explanation. We can simply accept that much of the Third World has many of the characteristics of dependency as described above; we can then ask how these features shape the kinds of environmental problems from which they suffer. In examining the question this way we will see that environmental issues arise in relation to all three sectors of economic dependency outlined earlier: manufacturing, mineral exploration and agriculture.

Finally in this section it is important to note one special factor which has had the effect of increasing the reality of the dependence of the Third World during the 1980s: the mounting problem of developing-country debt. In the last fifteen years many underdeveloped countries have become literally dependent on credit from the north to avoid insolvency. We will return to the impact of this factor in a later section.

MANUFACTURE, MINING AND POLLUTION IN THE THIRD WORLD

It is probably safe to say that all industrialization is accompanied by environmental damage. Certainly, the history of industrial development in the West is associated with the loss of woodland, with pollution of air and rivers and with problems of ill health resulting from quarrying and manufacture. Additionally, the energy needs of industry tend to encourage acid pollution in the atmosphere and, as we have seen, carbon dioxide emissions. Industrialization of the Third World is no exception. In some regards we might expect it to be less damaging than was the original Industrial Revolution: modern technologies are often cleaner and safer than their predecessors. On the other hand, some distinctively modern products are extremely damaging and the high productivity of contemporary industry places great demands on energy supply and is therefore likely to lead to intense pollution. But the situation is not as simple as this. In important ways, the dependent position of Third-World economies makes them susceptible to environmentally harmful industrialization.

Two factors work together to make this come about. The first is a 'pull' from the Third World. As described above, countries of the south often find themselves competing to attract investment from companies in the richer nations. They may try to succeed in this competition by offering favourable terms, such as lower wages, weaker unions, or tax exemptions. But they can also offer more relaxed environmental regulations and less strict environmental health provisions. For the sake of some access to industrial investment, they may be willing to risk the pollution of their natural environment. Sometimes, such measures may be justified in terms of the low level of existing pollution; the authorities may argue that the country's rivers can tolerate some discharge since Europe's rivers have survived hundreds of years of abuse. On other occasions, pollution is regarded as the price which has to be paid for modernization. Either way, these countries may offer themselves as pollution havens.

This tendency is matched by a 'push' factor. Some companies with successful but polluting businesses find it practically or economically undesirable to comply with the north's increasingly strict environmental regulations. They therefore seek out investment opportunities where the laws are less stringent or where the authorities do not enforce regulations, either because they cannot or because they do not care to. This investment strategy can be described as regulation flight.

Given the great diversity of Third-World countries it is not possible to present an account dealing with a 'typical' country, far less to deal with the whole of the south. But a useful composite picture can be derived from a range of examples. Early on, as Stott notes (1984, p. 28), warnings about the environmental hazards of industrialization were sometimes derided by officials from the Third World:

> Brazilian delegates at the 1972 U.N. Conference on the Human Environment proclaimed that it was their country's 'turn' to industrialize, and assured multinational corporations [TNCs] that it was alright [sic] to send this pollution down to Brazil so long as they sent the industries and the jobs that went with it.

Similar sentiments, this time attributed to an Irish politician keen to see his country's economy develop, are also noted by Leonard (1988, p. 126; see also Redclift 1984, pp. 45–8). These views are not confined to unguarded statements: Stott cites a brochure seeking to persuade companies to locate in an industrial complex in Trinidad. The text informs companies that '*In the absence* of legislation dealing with the discharge of effluents and other forms of pollution' intending investors have to convince the development authorities that the environmental impact has been properly assessed (1984, p. 30, emphasis added). In other words, there are no rules, and environmental protection is left to the discretion of an agency whose main job is to promote industrial development.

With this kind of encouragement many First-World companies, particularly TNCs, established more or less dirty industries in the south during the 1970s and 1980s. Critics noted the adverse, occasionally catastrophic, effects of this practice, effects vividly represented in the public mind by the deaths resulting from the escape of poisonous gas at the Union Carbide pesticide plant at Bhopal in India (Castleman and Purkavastha 1985). In some circles it became an orthodox belief that TNCs were systematically endangering the environment in the whole Third World, driven there precisely to avoid the high pollution control costs in the USA (for a sketch of this view see Michalowski and Kramer 1987, pp. 34–8).

Recently a more complex analysis of this phenomenon has begun to be spelled out. For one thing the effect of TNCs on the Third World is far from uniform. Their activities are highly concentrated. As Jenkins observes, eight states account for over half of the stock of direct foreign investment in the countries of the south (1987, pp. 13–14). Second, only some sorts of businesses are likely to be motivated to (re-)locate in the Third World. Leonard suggests that in some sectors (for example, pulp and paper industries) it has been relatively easy for firms in the north to improve domestic pollution control. By contrast, it is anticipated that chemical and mineral-processing industries would be attracted to regulation flight (Leonard 1988, pp. 92–3). A third consideration is that other issues may be of far greater importance in determining location decisions than the avoidance of pollution control costs. Labour costs or the price of raw materials may override the question of pollution (1988, pp. 83–6). Alternatively, companies may reckon that they can adapt technically to new pollution limits in the developed world; they may even calculate that they can remain in the north by evading new environmental laws (Levenstein and Eller 1985).

For all these reasons it is hard to determine how much companies' location decisions are guided by pollution related issues. Even if an exact computation of the expected economic costs and benefits could be done, some factors would still confound economic calculation. Companies wishing to remain in the north may face obstacles in addition to taxation and legal limitations on pollution: their operations may be disrupted by protest from a lobbying group or from a local community organization. Even within Europe, as we saw to be the case with the nuclear industry in Chapter 3, what is publicly accepted in one region may meet with strong protests elsewhere. Thus,

> when US companies, even those facing extreme pressure because of pollution problems at home, decide to build a plant abroad instead of in the United States, they do not necessarily do so because of differentials in pollution control costs or because governmental and public concern for the environment may cause delays in construction. (Leonard 1988, pp. 86–7)

This is as true for Europe or Japan as for the USA. Apparently, therefore, the suggestion that regulation flight alone would lead to vast changes in firms' location decisions is exaggerated.

All the same, even if the avoidance of pollution control costs does not drive TNCs to the Third World, once located there they 'remain legally free to expose the water, air, soil and bodies of workers to hazardous substances at rates higher than those allowed in their home countries' (Michalowski and Kramer 1987, p. 37). Even if they did not go to the Third World to pollute, the companies may be tempted to pollute once they are there. Of course, companies may choose to honour the same environmental standards as they observe in their home country, in which case they are likely to be in the vanguard of pollution control (see Berger 1987, p. 127). But if they are tempted to take advantage of the more relaxed regulations in the Third World or of the lack of enforcement, the threats they pose are likely to extend beyond the narrowly environmental. In other words there will be threats in addition to the environmental damage inflicted during the building of the plant and the discharges which subsequently emanate from it. TNCs may take advantage of weak laws protecting employees' health, enabling the firm to require (for example) prolonged exposure to chemicals or lengthy periods at microscopes, a practice which harms the eyesight of workers in the micro-electronics industry. On the other hand, companies may take the opportunity to continue to manufacture and to sell overseas products which have had to be withdrawn from the domestic market because they are a danger to consumers' health. In this context Michalowski and Kramer cite the case of a brand of children's sleepwear treated with a flame retardant chemical which was subsequently found to be a potential cause of cancer. The product was banned from sale in the USA but continued to be marketed elsewhere (1987, p. 38).

To examine how all these factors come together to shape pollution from manufacturing in the Third World we can consider two case-studies. The first concerns industrial development close to Mexico's border with the USA. This location was selected by the Mexican authorities as a site for industrial expansion because of its proximity to wealthy markets in the USA (Leonard 1988, pp. 144–6). The plants which have been attracted there tended to have several features in common: for example, the work conducted had a high labour intensity, moderate transport costs and consisted of a relatively self-contained stage in the overall production process. Plants which were already successfully established included textile and pottery workshops. The avoidance of pollution controls was not a major common feature in the industries in this zone. However, a proportion of the factories deal in asbestos products and other hazardous chemicals. Leonard concludes that this migration of environmentally harmful industries has not been explicitly favoured by the Mexican government, 'Nor has the crucial reason for the relocation in Mexico been the absence of work-place health controls in Mexico. The labor intensity of the products has been the decisive element on both accounts' (1988, p. 145). All the same, Mexico's desire for investment and industrialization has led it to welcome companies whose factories pollute the environment and damage workers' health. It is ironic that Mexico, which has no asbestos mines, should be importing asbestos pollution (Stott 1984, p. 29).

The second example is the city of Cubatão in southern Brazil, described by Ives (1985) and Stott (1984). Stott relates how the city has adopted a policy of welcoming TNCs' investment. Polluting Brazilian-owned companies have also set themselves up there. Although a comparative economic success, it is 'probably the dirtiest town in the world' (Stott 1984, p. 28).[3] The pollution has grave health effects, with life expectancy reduced to half of the national average and very high incidences of 'skin disease, cancer and bronchitis' (1984, p. 29). Air pollution affects not only the inhabitants' health but their physical environment. Stott reports that acid rain corrodes the corrugated iron roofing material which is in widespread use and even electricity pylons. Thus the economic benefits of industrialization are partly undermined by costs directly imposed by the resulting pollution.

As this example indicates, the encouragement of polluting industry can have disadvantages even at an economic level. While the industry may generate some profits and tax revenue for the country it is likely to impose high medical costs and to take its toll on infrastructural investment. Equally, areas with a strong potential for earnings through tourism – such as the Caribbean islands – may find that industrial effluents undermine tourist revenues by polluting seas or driving away attractive wildlife. The final ironic feedback is highlighted by Leonard. He claims that there is little evidence that healthy, growing industries are driven out of the USA by pollution control costs; they typically fund pollution control out of rising profits. The firms that are attracted overseas are likely to be ones for whose products there is no longer a great demand, possibly because they are growing obsolete or are perceived as hazardous. Sadly, from the point of view of the Third World, 'the flight of a few ailing industries from the United States is not likely to contribute in any significant way to the development of countries trying to build their industrial base' (Leonard 1988, p. 116).

In other words, those companies which do re-locate to the Third World for environmental reasons are almost bound to bring pollution and environmental health problems in their wake but are unlikely to yield large economic benefits.

So far in this section we have examined manufacturing investment, even though we observed earlier that many Third-World countries rely on the sale of minerals for a large share of their export earnings. However the two pictures are very similar, except that in this case indigenous companies, even nationalized ones, feature more frequently among the leading polluters. Let us begin with the Philippines where, as Susan George points out,[4] the existence of gold reserves seems to offer something of a lifeline for a poor and politically troubled country. One large mining area, Davao, has attracted tens of thousands of workers seeking an escape from poverty; the government too is keen to increase national output and state income. During the extraction process, mercury is used to dissolve out the gold from the ore. The gold is then recovered by heating the gold-mercury amalgam. Both processes are dangerous. In the latter case, the mercury vapours produced during heating are directly injurious to workers' health unless elaborate precautions are taken. Equally dangerous, during the extraction stage, mercury escapes into the environment, running into the soil and water courses. According to George, workers have established mining towns downstream of the extraction operations. The miners drink polluted water and eat local foods, themselves increasingly contaminated as the mercury spreads through the food chain.

Uranium mining, a vital activity in Niger's economy as we have seen, is also associated with considerable environmental dangers. Although the aim of mining is, of course, to remove the radioactive uranium, residual radioactive hazards are closely associated with the mining operation. The radioactive gas radon is emitted during mining and itself undergoes decay to produce polonium. Polonium is a rare, radioactive metal. Atoms of this metal appear spontaneously in the air of the mines as the radon gas naturally disintegrates. The polonium tends to attach itself to dust particles and can then easily be carried into miners' lungs, leading in many cases to lung cancer (Patterson 1976, p. 89). For its part, the uranium ore is often of such a low grade that over 99 per cent of mined material has to be discarded. These 'tailings' from the mines have to be stored somewhere, even though they too are radioactive to a slight degree. Deposited beside a river or close to a town, their health effects can be very serious. Patterson notes that in the 1960s, during the initial period of superpower enthusiasm for nuclear weapons, the mine tailings were so plentiful that they were used in filling around the foundations of buildings, 'including homes, schools and hospitals' even in the USA (1976, p. 90). Littered around the world, refuse from the mines will remain radioactive for thousands of years.

These two examples illustrate the dangers associated just with mining operations. Miners in poorer nations will tend to be protected by lower safety standards and enjoy lower levels of health education. There are also economic pressures to keep mining costs down in order to generate as much revenue as possible. This is true even though, as Jenkins notes, in the last two decades there has been a trend towards the nationalization of such resources in the Third World (1987, p. 11). But TNCs remain heavily involved in the area where mining and manufacture meet, in the mineral-processing industry. In this context, Jenkins cites the example of the production of aluminium from bauxite. Although Third-World bauxite sources have been used since the time of the First World War, processing was mostly retained in the developed world, taking advantage of economies of scale. However, the nations where the bauxite was mined wished to have more of the processing located there, hoping thereby to enjoy more of the profits. Many factors were important in deciding whether these countries attained this goal; the price of energy was particularly influential, favouring Third-World countries with hydro-electric power or fuel reserves. But another consideration was the fact that 'Pollution costs have also increased the capital costs of mining and processing facilities by as much as 25 per cent' (Jenkins 1987, p. 109). Still, the temptation to move to Third-World countries with less strict regulations has so far been largely offset by subsidies to the powerful corporations in the developed world.

A final example comes again from Mexico. Alongside their attempts to export manufactured goods to the USA, the Mexican authorities have aimed to improve their trade balance by restricting the export of unprocessed minerals. A rapid increase has accordingly taken place in Mexico's capacity to smelt copper, lead and zinc. This had led to increases in pollution not least because 'Mexican mineral processors, especially in the copper industry, operate smelters with much higher levels of sulfur dioxide emissions than those permitted in the United States' (Leonard 1988, p. 146). In this case, according to Leonard, pollution arises not so much because of a push from dirty northern industries but because of an interaction between the Third-World country's desire to have processing on its territory and its willingness to tolerate pollution from state-owned as well as private enterprises.

To conclude this section it is important to turn to two further ways in which industrialization poses an environmental threat to the Third World. The first of these was described in Chapter 1

As the countries of the north raise their own pollution control standards it becomes more complex and costly to dispose of waste, particularly hazardous and toxic waste. An attractive alternative is to ship it to a Third-World country where the controls are less stringent (Michalowski and Kramer 1987, pp. 37–8). West African countries, close to Europe and with low national incomes, became popular as destinations for some of the north's dangerous refuse. They were led to become involved in this trade for a number of reasons (Dowden 1988; Secrett 1988). Even if they charged far less than the market rate for disposal in the north, these nations found that dumping could be a profitable use for low-productivity land. The earnings were immediate and brought much-needed foreign exhange. In some cases, the importing nations' authorities have been misled about the nature of the waste or about the hazard it poses. In other cases judicious bribes have led officials to admit proscribed materials. Lastly, it is suggested that some of the importing countries' leaders may be rather careless of the health of (some of) their citizens; one can imagine how, in an ethnically divided country, the leaders of one faction may not be too distressed to see toxic waste buried in their opponents' region (Dowden 1988, p. 8).

The second particular threat arises from the spread of nuclear power generation to the Third World. We saw in Chapter 1 that nuclear energy offers to liberate countries from an exclusive reliance on fossil fuels; at the same time it is associated with profound environmental dangers. Commercial nuclear power is still uncommon in the underdeveloped world although many countries have research reactors (for an overview see Elsworth 1990, p. 284, and Kidron and Segal 1984, p. 16). One concern is that the economic and political dependence of Third-World nations means that they are liable to opt for nuclear plants under the influence of Western companies or development agencies. George gives a particularly chilling example of this possibility (1988, pp. 18–19). Under the former Marcos government, in 1976 the Philippines ordered a nuclear power station from the US firm Westinghouse for $2.1 billion. The country had to borrow to pay for this facility, a loan which, by 1987, was costing half a million dollars per day. Having taken out this loan and paid so much interest the country was then in an ambivalent position:

The reactor is ready to go; that it is not yet operating is perhaps just as well. The building site chosen is in the middle of the Pacific 'fire-rim' earthquake zone at the foot of a volcano. The International Atomic Energy Authority noted in a 1978 report that the choice of the Morong site in a zone of such high seismic activity was 'unique in the atomic industry' (George 1988, pp. 18–19).

By 1990 the Philippines had changed tack and was pinning energy hopes on new coal-fired power stations and geothermal energy projects. But these facilities are not yet in place and in early 1990 the country was facing an energy crisis. Extensive power cuts 'are crippling industry, discouraging foreign investment and increasing popular dissaffection with President Corazon Aquino's government' (*Guardian* 24 April 1990, p. 12). Meanwhile, repayments on the loan must continue. In this case, the Philippines' weak economic position, coupled with political dependency, has saddled the country with the financial and (some of) the environmental costs of nuclear power in the absence of any of the benefits.

In summary, the weakness and dependence of the Third World means that it is in a poor position to bargain over industrial investment. Underdeveloped countries can try to boost their competitive position by producing cheaply themselves or by offering firms a variety of methods for cost saving; low pollution control costs are just one method. While the invitation to pollute does not often seem to be the major factor in influencing TNCs' location decisions, the relaxed regulations lead to extensive environmental damage in the Third World by both foreign and indigenous enterprises. Ironically, the firms most commonly attracted by this opportunity are not the ones to which the Third World would ideally wish to appeal.

AGRIBUSINESS, FOOD AND THE ENVIRONMENT

The postwar transformation of Western agriculture was outlined in Chapter 1. Essentially, control over food production, processing and sales has increasingly passed into the hands of large companies. Many such companies, referred to as agribusinesses, are themselves TNCs, including Nestlé, Heinz and Del Monte. Other large TNCs with no apparent connection with food, such as ICI, are also involved since they produce fertilizers and pesticides as well as being engaged in the seed business. There are also farm equipment manufacturers. The influence of these companies in the Third World has a long history, dating from the end of the nineteenth century: 'The United Fruit Company was formed in 1899 and established its "Banana Empire" in Central America and the Caribbean before World War I' (Jenkins 1987, p. 5).

Many of the observations made in the last section would apply to transnational agribusinesses also. But there are three areas of their activities which deserve special attention. The first of these relates to characteristic features of agricultural production. In Third-World countries agriculture is generally the largest employer, and food for local consumption is often grown at low levels of productivity. Agribusinesses are attracted to the Third World because of its favourable climate: certain crops will only grow in the tropics, for example, while others, such as melons and strawberries, can be grown very advantageously there. But the crops which these companies wish to grow are not destined for the local market. Something like 98 per cent of the yield of luxury crops may be exported (Feder 1976, p. 424). These crops would be too expensive for the majority of local people and are, in any case, not selected for their nutritional value. Agribusinesses have attracted criticism for using the best land to grow crops for export (cash crops), thus leaving countries with the potential to feed themselves in need of food imports. In principle, the profits on the luxury items ought to be more than enough to allow the countries to buy in staple foodstuffs. However, once the food companies have taken their profits, charged for their agro-chemicals and their expertise, the sums may no longer add up (George 1990, pp. 23–38). In any case, this agricultural strategy undermines the Third-World countries' food independence.

The specifically environmental problem with this arrangement concerns the kinds of contract which agribusinesses are able to strike. Contracts may be of two general sorts: either the agribusiness buys land and employs local workers directly, or local farmers act as growers, retaining ownership of the land but raising crops in accordance with the company's wishes and selling to that company. Whichever system is adopted, the company's leading economic interest is in maximizing production, while the locals have an additional interest in retaining the fertility of the soils. Broadly speaking, the locals have only this land as an economic resource while the companies can move elsewhere if productivity starts to fall: 'Decreasing yields are no particular problem to the US investors because they can be offset by shifting strawberry plantations to new, fertile and clean soils which are abundantly available' (Feder 1976, p. 433). In consequence, agribusinesses – under competitive economic pressure – have tended to exploit the land as fully as possible, making extensive use of fertilizers and pesticides (George 1977, pp. 175–6). This leads both to degradation of the soil and to the spread of chemicals in water courses and the environment more generally.[5]

The question of the use of agro-chemicals leads directly into the second set of environmental problems associated with trans-national agribusiness. Underdeveloped countries tend to have fewer and weaker restrictions on these chemicals than does the north. In part, this is a question of the *manufacture* of these substances. With regard to manufacture, the analysis is essentially the same as that outlined in the last section; after all, the Union Carbide plant in Bhopal was producing pesticides. Leonard observes that some Mexican companies have moved into the manufacture of certain dangerous agro-chemicals that are in an anomalous legal position. Although their production in the USA is now forbidden these substances may still be used under exceptional circumstances (1988, p. 145); there is thus a demand for them in the USA but no domestic supply.

Apart from the conditions of manufacture, an important aspect of these agro-chemicals is the circumstances under which they are used. Unlike many other kinds of potentially harmful substances, agro-chemicals are almost bound to have a strong interaction with the environment. They are spread over fields or administered to animals and they can end up in the food consumed by people. The potential dangers were highlighted by some disastrous accidents in the 1970s, in particular a poisoning incident in Iraq, where hungry peasants made flour from seeds intended for planting; the seeds had been treated with highly toxic, mercury-based fungicides which caused many hundred deaths (Ives 1985, p. 181). Most concern has been expressed about more insidious problems. For example, agro-chemicals found to be hazardous in the north may continue to be used in the underdeveloped world for a number of reasons. Legal changes may be slow to come about or the replacement chemicals may be too costly for poor countries to afford; the substances may even continue in use as the result of deceitful practices (Castleman 1985, pp. 76–80). Given that pesticides are meant to cause biological harm of some sort, there is room for concern about the dose levels used and the conditions under which they are applied. Agricultural workers in the Third World may lack protective clothing (Castleman 1985, p. 77). Equally dangerous, if in the absence of adequate supervision or labelling or comprehension very high doses are applied, there is bound to be a run-off of chemicals into the environment. This will affect water courses, local wildlife and local people. By a final irony, cash crops from the Third World may find their way back to the north's markets even if they have been chemically treated in a way that would never be permitted in the north's domestic agriculture (see Weir and Shapiro 1981).

The third point in this section concerns technical innovation in agriculture. I described in Chapter 1 the arguments about the importance of the Third World's genetic resources, particularly in regard to the rain forests. While the majority of the world's genetic resources originate in underdeveloped countries, most of the scientific research on agricultural genetics has been conducted in the north. Plant breeding has been going on for centuries but recently the possibility of genetic engineering of agricultural species has arisen (see George 1990, pp. 109–38; Redclift 1989, pp. 185–98; and Yoxen 1983, pp. 144–80). It is easy to imagine potential benefits: crops could be developed with unusually high yields, with inbuilt disease resistance, or with a tolerance of drought. Yet, since much of the research is being carried out by companies in the private sector, they need to find ways of ensuring that a profit results from the new crops. One attractive possibility is to develop a crop which is specifically resistant to the company's own weed and pest control products. It would then be possible for farmers to buy the company's seeds and, by spraying at the correct time

with that company's agro-chemicals, eliminate everything but
the crop (George 1990, p. 120). The farmer would be tied
to the agribusiness company. Commentators such as George
have expressed various misgivings about this development, particularly because it threatens to make agriculture more capital
intensive and to concentrate more power in the hands of TNCs.
For our purposes, two main sorts of problem can be identified.
At first sight genetic engineering might appear to offer a route
away from the use of hazardous pesticides if, for example, pest
resistance can be inbred. However, crops which can tolerate a
particular herbicide may actually encourage the more extensive
use of agro-chemicals, thus burdening the environment even
more. Second, there are unknown dangers associated with the
introduction of engineered species into the wild. By definition
these are unnatural and their exact environmental consequences
can only be a matter of (more or less informed) speculation (see
Williams 1990b).[6]

DEBT AND AID: AN INTRODUCTION

Up to this point we have examined the environmental consequences of industrialization and economic development in the
Third World. In the last fifteen years these processes have been
subject to an additional influence: the vast growth of capital
flows to the Third World and the corresponding expansion of
debt repayments. Of course, capital has always moved between
the First and Third Worlds. From the outset, European countries
invested in, as well as benefitted from, their colonies. Later on,
TNCs transferred wealth to and from underdeveloped countries.
Funds have also long been available from two other important
sources. First, there are two major international institutions,
established at the same time in anticipation of the end of the
Second World War: the World Bank and the International
Monetary Fund (IMF). The IMF's intended function was to
make short-term loans to countries which were suffering from
balance of payments problems – that is, countries which tempo-
rarily found themselves with larger import bills than they could
finance through exports. The IMF would assist these countries
on condition that they took the approved steps to improve their

economic performance. For its part, the World Bank was primarily in the business of offering loans for development projects. Initially these loans were aimed at postwar reconstruction. The bank sought to be very prudent in its loans, scrutinizing the proposed projects very carefully for their economic viability.

The second source of funding is aid. Most aid comes from governments even though voluntary agencies such as Oxfam and Save the Children command a good deal of public support. First-World countries vary enormously in the amount of aid they supply although, inevitably, the largest economies have the most to offer (see Hayter 1989, p. 27). In 1986, Norway gave over 1 per cent of GNP in aid while the USA gave about a fifth of 1 per cent and the UK a little over a quarter. In cash terms the USA contributed the greatest amount. Official aid has attracted a great deal of criticism, as we shall see. In particular, it is claimed that aid is allocated not according to the need or the deserts of the recipient but with an eye to the economic or political returns to the donor (Hayter and Watson 1985, pp. 238–47; Yearley 1988, pp. 158–63). All the same, aid is an attractive form of funding because it consists of outright grants or of cheap loans. In principle, therefore, it can be used for projects which are vital to development but which do not yield immediate and obvious economic returns, such as the provision of schooling and medical facilities.

Changes in world banking during the 1970s fundamentally transformed the way that development finance was to be provided. To simplify, the background to these changes was as follows. After the sudden oil price rise in 1973 the oil-producing countries found themselves with unprecedented profits. Initially, as we saw in Chapter 1, the nations of the north were disturbed by the resulting increase in energy prices but they learned to economize on fuel and also began to sell many more manufactured goods to the oil-rich countries. The developed world's banks also benefited because it was to them that the oil producers turned to invest their new wealth (Lever and Huhne 1985, pp. 11–38). The only remaining problem was for the banks to find good investment opportunities which would pay them a return, allowing them to profit on the deal. The solution adopted by many banks was to invest in parts of the Third World which seemed to offer the prospect of rapid industrialization: countries such as Mexico, well placed for trade with the USA and blessed with some oil wealth, and Brazil, rich in natural resources and apparently ripe for economic 'take off'. Third-World states usually found this opportunity attractive. They had ambitious development plans and welcomed the access to more plentiful funds. Not only was there more money than had been supplied by aid and the World Bank, the money was more freely available. Loans from commercial banks had fewer restrictions attached than had earlier forms of funding.

For a while it seemed that everyone would benefit: oil producers received good interest, banks earned good commissions and the Third World had access to new resources. But by the turn of the decade problems were beginning to appear. A slump in world trading reduced the markets for Third-World countries' goods, including their exports of primary materials. At the same time, the USA was beginning to run a trade deficit. It needed to borrow money in order to finance the costs of being a superpower; this forced up interest rates. Finally, it became clear that the loans to the Third World were not generating the size of returns that was wanted. In turn, this last problem was due to three factors. The banks and the recipient countries were not necessarily skilled in development planning. Therefore many of the investments did not meet with the anticipated success. Second, in some cases the leaders and social elites in the underdeveloped world had abused the loans. Rather than invest the money in economically productive ways, they had salted it away in Swiss bank accounts or spent it on holiday villas. Lastly, the lenders themselves had behaved irresponsibly. They had to keep finding investments and accordingly became less and less discriminating. Bank employees found themselves looking for borrowers to whom they could give loans rather than waiting for well-documented proposals to come to them (George 1988, pp. 30–3). Lever and Huhne cite the practices of French and American banks in Gabon (an oil and manganese exporter in west central Africa). Their activities resulted in

> a triumphal highway linking the airport and the presidential palace, a hotel sector with occupancy rates resembling those of a seaside resort in mid-winter, a fleet of commerical jet aircraft, enlarged government buildings and one of the world's

least economical railways, built against the World Bank's planning advice. (1985, p. 59)

None of these projects would ever earn enough to repay the loan.

By the early 1980s the recipients of the loans were earning less from their investments but having to repay interest at higher rates. In some countries, such as the Philippines and Nicaragua, new governments had come into power, facing huge debt repayments even though their predecessors had squandered or stashed away the borrowed money. The end of this global spending spree was marked in 1982 when Mexico announced that it was unable to repay the interest on its loans (George 1988, pp. 40–4). Since that date the debt problem has been managed but not solved. None of the banks singly can resolve the issue. Although they mostly acknowledge that the majority of debts will never be repaid and have made allowances for that possibility, they are unwilling to excuse any of the debtors. They say this would be unfair on those countries which have continued with repayments.

The IMF has moved into this policy vacuum and assumed a powerful position. It has played a large part in setting the conditions under which debtor countries have been granted new loans or concessions to cover their repayment obligations. Its remedies have usually included a decrease in public expenditure (on welfare programmes and so on), a devaluation of the currency to encourage international competitiveness and a re-orientation of the economy towards exports. Each of these measures is intended to decrease the amounts debtors spend at home and to increase their external earnings; in both ways they should be better able to meet their outgoings.

These measures have met with a good deal of criticism. In the countries concerned, the IMF's policies have sometimes been associated with public protests and riots (in Jordan and Venezuela in early 1989 for example (*Time* 31 July 1989, pp. 30–3)). Commentators such as George argue that the IMF's measures have a disproportionate effect on the poor in the Third World, removing funds for such items as food subsidies and welfare benefits, while the rich are protected by their foreign bank accounts. The Third World's poor seem to have suffered in order that the banking system could be preserved with as little disruption as possible (see Lever and Huhne 1985, pp. 64–83). In summary, George claims that these measures increase differences between the rich and the poor, making the poor worse off (1988, pp. 119–40). This claim contrasts strongly with Berger's insistence (1987, pp. 132–6) that contact with international capitalism tends to be good for the world's poorest people. The debt problem seems to have introduced a very real dependence into north–south relations and – whatever the rights and wrongs of dependency theory – to have made the notion of underdevelopment look only too realistic.

DEBT AND THE ENVIRONMENT

A discussion of the social, economic and political implications of debt could detain us for a long time but it is important to turn to the environmental consequences of this problem. These fall into two categories: the results of the projects financed with the loans and the impact of the remedial steps taken once the debt crisis broke. As we have seen, the loans were granted for a wide range of types of spending, not all of which were closely allied to development (for example Third-World spending on arms rose markedly in the 1970s (Lever and Huhne 1985, p. 47)). But, among those monies destined for development projects, there was a tendency to support grandiose projects offering (or purporting to offer) rapid industrial development. Environmental impact studies were usually not a major part of the plans for these projects. Of course, for much of the 1970s, environmental considerations failed to rank very highly in planning policy even in the developed world, so this was probably only to be expected. But as an example of the use of these loans we can take the case of the Tucurui dam in north-eastern Brazil, to the south of the Amazon delta. In the construction of this dam, begun in 1976, hundreds of thousands of hectares of forest were destroyed and local peoples and wildlife were evicted. This case is especially notorious because much of the forest was not cleared before flooding began even though, under an earlier scheme, the trees had been sprayed with a defoliant (dioxin). Drums of this toxic chemical were also allegedly left in the submerged area (George 1988, p. 157). The potential environmental impact of the escape of dioxin into water courses is clearly horrific.

On turning to the consequences of the response to the debt problem we find that they are, if anything, more far-reaching. For one thing, the loans are denominated in dollars so that foreign exchange has to be raised to pay them off. This has led to a great emphasis on exports. It therefore encourages cash cropping and mining projects – even the acceptance of toxic waste cargoes. And because there is a need to do these things as profitably as possible, these environmentally risky developments are undertaken with minimum attention to conservation. Probably the most graphic example here involves the Brazilian rain forests. In order to raise export earnings it makes a certain sense to use good land in Brazil to raise cash crops, notably soya beans and beef cattle; after all, agriculture contributes half of the country's export earnings (Searle 1987, p. 61). Wealthy ranchers tend to have dominated this trade and they require few labourers per hectare (Gradwohl and Greenberg 1988, pp. 41–3). But cash cropping of this sort precludes land reform and thus leaves the authorities with the problem of the rural poor, a problem they have been tempted to try to solve by encouraging the poor to settle virgin land in the rain forests (George 1988, p. 165). One area in which this policy was systematically adopted was the north-west region of Brazil, in and around the state of Rondonia (Searle 1987, p. 62). A set of colonization projects was formulated and even attracted assistance from the World Bank (a commitment the bank now apparently regrets (Guest 1989)). However, as we saw in Chapter 1, the rain forest is generally not suited to agricultural development and many of the settlers drawn to Rondonia had to keep clearing more land just to make a living. This has led to ill-controlled destruction of the forest and conflict between settlers and native forest dwellers. Searle (1987, pp. 107–10) argues that the responsibility for these problems must be shared between the Brazilian authorities and those who organize financial and trade links with the north. The 'mal-development' (George 1988, p. 14) of this area is closely bound to international economic and political dependency.

So far we have looked at the possibility that a country may try to meet its debt repayments by intensifying its existing economic practices, by raising more cash crops for example. There is an alternative route which it may attempt: it may turn to new investments, hoping to use the profits from these to meet its repayments. This approach has won support among advocates of growth and has been backed by the World Bank and other Western agencies. One example of this strategy is the Grande Carajas project, based on the power supplied from the Tucurui dam. The project consists of a series of schemes exploiting local ore deposits, notably gold and iron ore (see Gradwohl and Greenberg 1988, p. 37; Schwarz 1989a). These ores are both mined and processed locally. Although the project has been estimated to cost $62 billion (about half the country's 1987 debt (Hayter 1989, p. 10)), the idea is that its eventual profits should help meet the costs of Brazil's repayments. It has received funding from a wide variety of sources; among them, the World Bank has sometimes been singled out for criticism because of its involvement. Environmentalists are concerned about the extent of open-cast mining and the associated plant but, more than anything else, they are worried by the development of aluminium smelters and iron furnaces powered by charcoal, itself produced by burning rain forest. As Pearce points out, the World Bank should not be blamed for this aspect of the project:

> The World Bank did not fund the smelters . . . Japan's International Cooperation Agency, a cornerstone of its aid programme, devised the wider economic development plan for Carajas, and in particular proposed firing blast furnaces with charcoal. Japanese markets will receive the cheap iron, steel and aluminium. (1990)

In order to gain the maximum economic benefit from this costly project the Brazilians are led to accept great ecological damage in the heart of the rain forests. This graphically represents the environmental dangers inherent in trying to trade one's way out of debt.

The third way in which responses to debt may have an impact on environmental protection is through reductions in state expenditure. By and large, environmental protection will only be carried out by state agencies or by non-governmental organizations funded by charities. A country's indebtedness is likely to decrease charitable giving while the IMF's insistence that state spending be cut has meant there is even less money for conservation programmes. Thus, even where the Brazilian state has sought to establish rain forest reserves there is 'no money to hire guards. The Brazilian Amazon, half as big as Europe, employs a total of 500 forest guards to keep off marauding gold diggers, encroaching loggers and illegal settlers' (Schwarz 1989a). Even when Third-World countries wish to address environmental problems they may find that debt robs them of the resources to do so. George notes that Bolivians have responded to their debt problems by resuming the trade in endangered wildlife (1988, p. 167).

AID, INTERNATIONAL INSTITUTIONS AND ENVIRONMENTAL PROTECTION

International debt, chiefly from commercial banks, now exceeds a trillion (a million million) dollars and clearly dwarfs other capital flows. But despite their smaller scale, monies supplied through aid and from the World Bank continue to have practical and symbolic importance. The bank's judgements have an influence on the policies of commercial lenders while aid can bypass debt problems. A brief review of the environmental consequences of these two sources of funding is thus called for.

Although the World Bank has been much criticized for its involvement in environmentally harmful projects, its president, Barber Conable, announced a greening of its attitudes in 1987 (*The Independent* 7 May 1987, p. 8). Henceforward, he claimed, the bank would not be a part of the problem but part of the solution. On account of its size and the complexities of its environmental problems, Brazil is seen as a test case for the bank. Certainly the bank drew some praise – or at least avoided further criticism – in 1989 when it withdrew support for a vast energy programme after the Brazilian authorities had sought to include their nuclear projects within the programme (Guest 1989). In the same spirit, the bank has reversed its attitude to the Rondonia settlement schemes by relaxing its demands for annual economic growth and by seeking to direct settlers towards sustainable agriculture (Guest 1990). Such moves are likely to be assisted by the public support for environmental protection given by the Brazilian president, Fernando Collor, who assumed office in 1990. The bank can certainly be expected to become more environmentally sensitive but its commitment – together with that of the IMF – to manage the debt problem will mean that economic growth has to remain its principal, overall objective.

If the World Bank is hamstrung by commercial imperatives, perhaps aid can be more effective. In many cases it seems not. For example, a National Audit Office (1990) report on a decade of UK aid to India disclosed that aided projects 'had caused dangerous pollution, the export of banned pesticides and civil unrest between local people and mine-owners' (*Guardian* 31 January 1990, p. 24). In her comprehensive review of British aid and the environment Hayter develops this point (1989, pp. 51–178). She is critical of UK aid for two principal reasons. First, aid distribution increasingly shadows IMF policy. Those countries which implement the IMF's programmes of adjustment to debt are rewarded with aid; those which do not are denied it. In this way aid tends to reinforce the environmentally harmful responses to debt which were outlined in the last section. Second, a large proportion of UK aid is 'tied': around two-thirds (1989, p. 26). In other words, aid is given on condition that it is used to buy British goods or services. The UK is far from alone in adopting this practice although it uses it to an uncommonly large degree. Such a policy inevitably shapes Third-World countries' development plans. For example, a country may opt for a single large dam for which support is forthcoming (since it can be built by a British firm) rather than seek alternatives which will not be aided. This leads to a preference for large-scale, high technology projects which tend to be environmentally intrusive.

The impact of aid can be very far-reaching as we saw earlier in the discussion of the Grande Carajas schemes. Until recently Japan was a relatively small donor of aid, restricting its activities largely to Asia. But with the increase in its trade surplus and pressure from the USA for it to assume a larger global role, Japan has boosted its aid budget and assumed a bigger involvement in the IMF (*Guardian* 27 September 1988, p. 9; 7 April 1989, p. 37). There is a fear among environmental campaigners that those countries which are expanding their aid programmes have their own economic interests very much at heart. Pearce cites one North American campaigner who warns of the Japanese 'addiction to large high-tech projects and their blindness to the environmental effects' (1990). Such fears may be exaggerated but they do indicate that, even if aid grows in the near future, its environmental consequences cannot be guaranteed to be favourable.

CONCLUDING DISCUSSION

In this chapter I have tried to set the environmental problems facing the Third World in the context of these countries' pursuit of social and economic development. In other words, I have accepted the view, outlined at the start of this chapter, that there are many systematic connections binding together the environmental challenges that confront the underdeveloped world. It might appear that by adopting this approach I have been led to look away from the certain international issues – in particular, the greenhouse effect and the conservation of the ozone layer – which are capturing worldwide attention. I do not mean to underestimate the importance of these issues. Rather, my argument is that they too should be examined in the light of the economic and political factors which shape industrial development and government policy in the Third World.

The global environmental threats, such as those arising from ozone depletion, are clearly alarming. They understandably command public interest. Their public profile is likely to be further raised, both by politicians – who like to associate themselves with a major issue in order to demonstrate their green credentials – and the media – which need arresting stories (see Lowe and Flynn 1989, p. 269). But I suggest that it makes less sense to treat these issues as a special category of problem (as 'ecological' problems) than to analyse them in a broader context, a context including indebtedness, huge differences in wealth and great inequalities of political power. To adopt only a narrow focus is to invite the acceptance of certain double standards. For example, we saw in Chapter 1 that the industrialization of the Third World would necessitate a large increase in carbon dioxide emissions. While politicians in the First World may be anxious to ally themselves with moves to curb increases in atmospheric carbon dioxide, they are far less keen to see their own countries' emissions cut sufficiently to permit a rapid rise in electricity generation in the Third World. Double standards can be seen to be at play in a far subtler way also. Western leaders can hardly urge Third-World governments to be more ecologically responsible and to carry out more environmental monitoring at the same time as Western financial policies oblige them to cut public sector employment. As I described in Chapter 3, international agreements are currently very important in trying to deal with environmental threats. If such agreements are to be credibly extended to the countries of the underdeveloped world, they will need to take account of the economic aspect of environmental hazards.

The interpretation which I have offered of the connection between ecological problems and dependency or underdevelopment does not require a resolution of the debate over the status of dependency theory. For one thing, it is clear that there are extensive environmental problems even in those countries which appear to be escaping from underdevelopment. For example, Taiwan is reported to have a 'monumental pollution problem', ranging from contamination from untreated sewage, through illegal dumping of toxic materials, to unregulated discharges from many factories (*Financial Times* 13 October 1989, p. 4). I have also several times mentioned the ecological destruction in the Second World. In part this came about because the pursuit of industrial growth and development was so remorseless and yet so narrowly interpreted; in part because some regions of the Warsaw Pact countries were effectively underdeveloped by their core areas. Loosely speaking, one might say the Warsaw Pact governments exploited their regions in place of their colonies. More recently, as the West grew wealthier and more concerned about its own environment, Second-World countries have begun to trade environmental hazard for hard currency. Thus, in 1989 East Germany took nearly 5 million tonnes of refuse, including some hazardous waste, from Western nations, notably the Federal Republic (*Time* 9 April 1990, p. 27). The close connection between dependency and certain forms of environmental problem can therefore be accepted as an empirical generalization, even if the standing of dependency theory is still in dispute.

Two further points can be addressed once we have accepted this generalization. The first relates to the practical significance of concerns about the environment. As I mentioned in the Introduction, some critics have argued that concern for the environment diverts attention from social and political inequalities (see the views described in Rüdig 1986, p. 379). The evidence presented in this chapter indicates that ecological threats in the Third World are neither superficial nor a distraction from pressing social problems. Even apart from the possible inherent value of nature conservation in the Third World, ecological issues are of central importance to the health of ordinary citizens and to the prospects for long-term economic development. Ecological issues can no longer be dismissed, whatever one's views on the development needs of dependent countries.

The second point relates directly to the question of economic growth. In Chapter 4 I outlined the current debate about the compatibility or otherwise of growth and of greening. As depicted in Chapter 4, this debate was primarily conducted between groups in the developed world. Some argued that we could continue with reformed economic expansion while others, like Porritt, argued for the abandonment of growth. Seen in a global perspective, this debate takes on a new urgency. One can ask, can the countries of the Third World ever hope to attain Western standards of wealth and consumption? Some clearly believe that they can, or at least, that they should try. In the study described earlier in this chapter, Berger defined development as 'the process by which people in the poorer countries *are to reach* the levels of material life achieved in the countries of advanced industrial capitalism' (1987, p. 116, emphasis added). Supporters of dependency theory would clearly disagree with Berger; their argument would be that such a goal is unrealistic because exploitation tends to hinder these nations' growth. But there is an additional argument: namely, that the global ecosystem simply could not sustain all the world's people consuming at the Western rate. The planet would soon be exhausted and polluted. For this reason, Caldwell has described the West as 'overdeveloped' (1977, pp. 98–138): it has a standard of consumption that simply could not be enjoyed worldwide.

Although in the short term Caldwell might have much in common with dependency theorists, his long-term objectives would be significantly different.

As we saw in Chapter 4, the kinds of argument advanced by Caldwell cannot be fully evaluated in abstract terms. This is because one can point to some sorts of growth which bring no net increase in pollution (Pezzey 1989). But arguments such as those put forward by Caldwell need to be taken into account when policies for the Third World are being assessed. Certainly his analysis would lead to scepticism about the global merits of one policy option we have examined: the idea that indebted Third-World countries should try to trade their way out of debt through a programme of concerted economic growth.

The final point to be made in this chapter is that, despite the severity of the Third World's environmental problems and the forces which lead to their perpetuation, there are some encouraging developments. For one thing some aid agencies, especially small-scale and (often) non-governmental groups, are beginning to incorporate ecological projects in their programmes (for a review see Conroy and Litvinoff 1988). There is growing expertise and experience in the sustainable management of tropical rain forests and other endangered habitats (Gradwohl and Greenberg 1988, pp. 173–7). Much hope has also been invested in the so-called 'debt-for-nature' swaps, according to which wealthy Western environmental groups use their funds to buy part of the dollar debts of Third-World countries. Since the banks do not believe that the loans will ever be redeemed in full, they are willing to pass on the loans at a discounted price: in 1987, an environmental group purchased $650,000 of Bolivian debt for only $100,000 (George 1988, p. 168). The idea is that the environmentalists then allow the debtor country to pay off the loan in local currency, the resulting money being used to purchase rain forest, which is set aside as a nature reserve. Some money is also usually retained to pay for wardens and for the reserve's upkeep.

Such schemes are not without their difficulties. It is hard to guarantee the continued integrity of the reserve; as we saw in Chapter 2, even in the UK designated sites are still sometimes lost to developers. No country is likely to make an unconditional commitment to maintaining a reserve. Moreover, the notoriously high inflation can eat away at the funds out of which wardens and reserve maintenance are paid. However, these swaps can form an important part of environmental protection programmes. Pressure on Western governments and official agencies needs to be maintained if these programmes are to have any success. Such pressure is likely to be made more effective by the last development I wish to list: increased co-operation between those Western pressure groups which work in the environmental area (such as FOE) and those which work for development (such as Oxfam). In the near future we can expect to see these groups making overlapping social problem claims and working together to lobby governments, international bodies and agencies such as the World Bank and the IMF.

NOTES

1   These figures come from the early 1980s, before the problems of international debt – to be discussed later in the chapter – aggravated the plight of the south.

2   In the whole of South and Central America only Brazil, Mexico and Argentina have GDPs greater than the economic value of General Motors' sales; see Jenkins 1987, p. 9.

3   Recent disclosures about environmental damage in Eastern Europe may offer candidates (such as the Romanian 'black town' of Copsa Mica) to rival Cubatão; see *Time* 9 April 1990, p. 24. Dirty industry in Romania is also discussed by Leonard (1988, pp. 147–53).

4   These details are derived from the television programme based on Susan George's work, called 'A Fate Worse than Debt', presented by her and broadcast on BBC2 on 28 December 1989.

5   I have restricted myself to the environmental impact of agribusiness. Other areas of activity have also attracted criticism, including the use of agricultural resources in the Third World to produce pet foods for the north or to grow non-food items like flowers; see George 1977, pp. 172–3 and Warnock 1987, pp. 129–50. A useful, introductory analysis of the social and environmental cost of food items grown in the Third World can be found in North 1986.

6   These issues were addressed in a BBC2 'Horizon' programme on genetic engineering and food, broadcast on 12 February 1990 and entitled 'Guess What's Coming to Dinner'. The programme made the point that Third-World states may have difficulty in controlling the release of genetically engineered organisms in their territory; it cited the case of an engineered rabies vaccine which had been used experimentally on cattle in Argentina.

Social science and the green case

Throughout this book I have been making – mostly implicitly – one central claim: that social science can make a significant contribution to understanding the green case. I suggest that this is true in two ways. At one level, social science is important to our appreciation of the green case precisely because there are major social, political and economic aspects to current environmental issues. Although most environmental problems are problems of the natural world and accordingly demand expertise in the natural sciences, this demand is by no means exclusive. In the examples we have studied, it has been clear that social conditions have contributed to bringing about ecological problems and that social change is necessary for their solution. This is as true for the case of endangered animal species as it is for attempts to arrest the depletion of the ozone layer. Nowhere is this connection of more vital importance than in relation to the Third World where, as we saw in the last chapter, concern about the environment is inseparable from questions of industrial investment and international finance.

In principle at least, this part of my claim would probably not be widely challenged. All the same, social science has not often been brought to the centre of the environmental debate. In part, this stems from the importance of the scientific aspects of ecological problems. The need for the skills of botanists, of engineers, of oceanographers and so on is readily recognized. As we saw in Chapters 1 and 2, much conservation activity arose out of a tradition of scientific work on the natural environment. It is tempting to suppose that such expertise alone will be sufficient for the resolution of current environmental difficulties. My argument is that it will not. It will plainly not suffice for policy making in relation to the developing world where technical considerations are typically dwarfed by economic ones. Equally true is that it is insufficient even in the industrialized world since the majority of decisions affecting our environment are made through the economic logic of markets or the competitive logic of the political process; most such decisions are most definitely not made by an appeal to disinterested technical expertise.

My call for greater recognition of the potential contribution of the social sciences is strengthened by the second part of my argument: that the social sciences already contain theoretical analyses which can readily be used to study the green case. I can briefly give three illustrative examples from the preceding chapters. There is first the tradition of analyses of the Third World in terms of dependency and underdevelopment. We saw in Chapter 5 how certain environmental problems were typical and symptomatic of dependent economies. In large part, these problems arose from that dependency. For example, there are structural pressures on developing countries which encourage them to have fewer and weaker environmental regulations than do First-World nations; this generalization was borne out in the examples we considered. The second tradition of analysis which can be employed in studying the green case comes from the sociology of scientific knowledge. I called on this approach in Chapter 4 to understand the weaknesses – as well as the more obvious strengths – which result from the green movement's dependence on scientific authority. Lastly, I have drawn on theories about social movements and social problems in order to understand why the green movement has evolved into its present shape – how, for example, the natural history background of the RSNC decisively influenced the basis of conservation policy in the UK. Other branches of social scientific theory could readily be added to this list: for example, political sociology, the study of pressure groups, or theories of the policy-making process. I believe that the social sciences enable us to understand the rise and the composition of the green movement and to anticipate sources of opposition to the green case. There should be increased social scientific study of the green case; more important, green practitioners and activists should be encouraged to turn more frequently to social scientists.

There is one leading factor which, I believe, accounts for a certain distance between social scientists and participants in environmental debates: the problem of objectivity. Social science can easily be undermined by partisanship. On the other hand, environmental activists tend to argue that 'if you are not part of the solution, you are part of the problem' (Cockburn 1990). The resulting tension can be illustrated by referring to theories about the 'social construction' of social problems, described in Chapter 2. For the sake of objectivity, analysts of social problems suspend judgement about the correctness of various social problem claims. They argue that the social processes of persuasion, of moral entrepreneurship, are essentially similar no matter how profound or how banal the cause. I adopted this agnostic stance, most specifically in Chapters 2 and 4. It appears to me that such disinterest is essential. It allows us to explain in an objective way the success of organizations such as the RSPB and Greenpeace; it also permits us to identify those parts of the natural environment which have benefited from their attentions. But to show that a social problem has been socially constructed is not to undermine or debunk it; both valid and invalid social problem claims have to be constructed. The detachment required for social science should not become an excuse for cynical inaction. I hope that readers of this text will be motivated to find out more about environmental problems and about the groups which are publicizing them. I hope too that they will make their own assessments of these groups' claims and start to act on their judgements.

Bibliography

Allaby, M. (1989), *Green Facts* 2nd edn (London: Hamlyn).

Allen, R. (1990), *Guests of the Nation: Chemical Multinationals and the Pollution of Ireland* (London: Earthscan).

Appleton, L. (1989), 'Trade–off', *BBC Wildlife*, vol. 7, no. 8, pp. 504–5.

Apter, D., and Sawa, N. (1984), *Against the State: Politics and Social Protest in Japan* (Cambridge, Mass.: Harvard University Press).

Baker, S. (1990), 'The evolution of the Irish ecology movement', in W. Rüdig (ed.), *Green Politics* (Edinburgh: Edinburgh University Press).

Barnes, B. (1985), *About Science* (Oxford: Blackwell).

Becker, H. S. (1973), *Outsiders* (New York: Free Press).

Benton, S. (1989), 'Turning green', *New Statesman and Society*, 23 June, pp. 10–11.

Berger, P. L. (1987), *The Capitalist Revolution* (Aldershot, Hants.: Wildwood House).

Bornstein, S. E. (1988), 'The Greenpeace affair and the peculiarities of French politics', in A. S. Markovits and M. Silverstein (eds), *The Politics of Scandal: Power and Process in Liberal Democracies* (New York: Holmes & Meier), pp. 91–121.

Bosquet, M. (1977), *Capitalism in Crisis and Everyday Life* (Brighton: Harvester).

Brown, M., and May, J. (1989), *The Greenpeace Story* (London: Dorling Kindersley).

Boyle, S., and Ardill, J. (1989), *The Greenhouse Effect: a Practical Guide to the World's Changing Climate* (London: Hodder & Stoughton).

Brunner, E. (1988), 'The big beef about jabs', *Guardian*, 14 September, p. 23.

Buerk, M. (1989), 'Poland's lethal legacy', *Observer Magazine*, 12 November, pp. 50–5.

Bürklin, W. P. (1983), 'Ansatzpunkte einer sozialstrukturellen Verankerung der neuen sozialen Bewegung', paper given at the congress of the German Political Science Association, Mannheim.

Button, J. (1989), *How to be Green* (London: Century).

Byrne, P. (1989), 'Great Britain: the "Green Party"', in F. Müller–Rommel (ed.), pp. 101–11.

Caldwell, M. (1977), *The Wealth of Some Nations* (London: Zed).

Castleman, B. I. (1985), 'The double standard in industrial hazards', in J. H. Ives (ed.), *The Export of Hazard* (London: Routledge & Kegan Paul), pp. 60–89.

Castleman, B. I. and Purkavastha (1985), 'The Bhopal disaster as a case study in double standards', in J. H. Ives (ed.), *The Export of Hazard* (London: Routledge & Kegan Paul), pp. 213–23.

Cockburn, A. (1990), 'The green racket', *New Statesman and Society*, 13 April, pp. 22–3.

Collingridge, D., and Douglas, J. (1984), 'Three models of policy making', *Social Studies of Science*, vol. 14, pp. 343–70.

Collins, H. (1988), 'Public experiments and displays of virtuosity: the core–set revisited', *Social Studies of Science*, vol. 18, pp. 725–48.

Conroy, C., and Litvinoff, M. (1988), *The Greening of Aid: Sustainable Livelihoods in Practice* (London: Earthscan).

Cope, D. (1989a), 'Sustainable development – the Pearce report', *UK CEED Bulletin*, vol. 25, pp. 6–7.

Cope, D. (1989b), 'Government collects views on eco–labelling', *UK CEED Bulletin*, vol. 26, pp. 8–9.

Cotgrove, S. (1982), *Catastrophe or Cornucopia: The Environment, Politics and the Future* (Chichester: Wiley).

Cotgrove, S., and Duff, A. (1980), 'Environmentalism, middle class radicalism and politics', *Sociological Review*, vol. 28, pp. 333–51.

Cotgrove, S., and Duff, A. (1981), 'Environmentalism, values and social change', *British Journal of Sociology*, vol. 32, pp. 92–110.

Cramer, J. (1987), *Mission–Orientation in Ecology: the Case of Dutch Fresh–Water Ecology* (Amsterdam: Rodopi).

Dixon, J. A., James, D. E., and Sherman, P. B. (1989), *The Economics of Dryland Management* (London: Earthscan).

Dobson, A. (1990), *Green Political Thought* (London: Unwin Hyman).

Dotto, L., and Schiff, H. (1978), *The Ozone War* (New York: Doubleday).

Dowden, R. (1988), 'Bribes and poverty that are poisoning Africa', *The Independent*, 17 June, p. 8.

Elkington, J., and Burke, T. (1987), *The Green Capitalists* (London: Gollancz).

Elkington, J., and Hailes, J. (1988), *The Green Consumer Guide* (London: Gollancz).

Elliot, R., and Gare, A. (eds) (1983), *Environmental Philosophy* (Milton Keynes: Open University Press).

Elsworth, S. (1990), *A Dictionary of the Environment* (London: Paladin).

Erlichman, J. (1988), 'BSE: a cow disease to beef about', *Guardian*, 11 July, p. 10.

Everest, D. (1989), 'Latest position on the science of ozone depletion', *UK CEED Bulletin*, vol. 26, p. 18.

Eyerman, R., and Jamison, A. (1989), 'Environmental knowledge as an organizational weapon: the case of Greenpeace', *Social Science Information*, vol. 28, pp. 99–119.

Feder, E. (1976), 'How agribusiness operates in underdeveloped agricultures', *Development and Change*, vol. 7, pp. 413–43.

Ferriman, A. (1989), 'Food dangers – how the lid was kept on', *The Observer*, 10 September, p. 9.

Friends of the Earth (UK) (1989), 'Recycled paper day of action', campaign material.

Friends of the Earth (UK)/*Observer Magazine* (1989), 'Your tap water, pure or poisoned', *Observer Magazine*, 6 August, pp. 16–24.

Gandy, O. H. (1982), *Beyond Agenda Setting* (Norwood, NJ: Ablex).

George, S. (1977), *How the Other Half Dies* (Harmondsworth: Penguin).

George, S. (1988), *A Fate Worse than Debt* (Harmondsworth: Penguin).

George, S. (1990), *Ill Fares the Land* (Harmondsworth: Penguin).

Gourlay, K. A. (1988), *Poisoners of the Seas* (London: Zed).

Gradwohl, J., and Greenberg, R. (1988), *Saving the Tropical Forests* (London: Earthscan).

Gribbin, J. (1988), *The Hole in the Sky* (London: Corgi).

Guest, I. (1989), 'Greenback to front', *Guardian*, 15 September, p. 21.

Guest, I. (1990), 'The Rambo factor', *Guardian*, 2 February, p. 27.

Hammond, N. (1983), 'The Royal Society for the Protection of Birds', in R. Hickling (ed.), *Enjoying Ornithology: A Celebration of Fifty Years of the British Trust for Ornithology, 1933–1983* (Calton, Staffs.: Poyser), pp. 158–64.

Harrison, D. (1988), *The Sociology of Modernization and Development* (London: Unwin Hyman).

Hays, S. P. (1987), *Beauty, Health and Permanence: Environmental Politics in the United States, 1955–85* (New York: Cambridge University Press).

Hayter, H. (1989), *Exploited Earth: British Aid and the Environment* (London: Earthscan).

Hayter, T., and Watson, C. (1985), *Aid: Rhetoric and Reality* (London: Pluto).

Heald, G., and Wybrow, R. J. (1986), *The Gallup Survey of Britain* (London: Croom Helm).

Hecht, S., and Cockburn, A. (1989a), 'Defenders of the Amazon', *New Statesman and Society*, 23 June, pp. 16–21.

Hecht, S., and Cockburn, A. (1989b), *The Fate of the Forest: Developers, Destroyers and Defenders of the Amazon* (London: Verso).

Hoogvelt, A. (1982), *The Third World in Global Development* (London: Macmillan).

Horsfall, J. (1990), 'The hijack of reason', *Guardian*, 20 April, p. 25.

Irvine, S. (1989), 'Beyond green consumerism', *Friends of the Earth Discussion Paper 1* (London: FOE).

Irwin, A. (1990), 'Acid pollution and public policy: the changing climate of environmental decision–making', in M. Radojevic and R. Harrison (eds), *Atmospheric Acidity: Sources, Consequences and Abatement* (Amsterdam: Elsevier).

Ives, J. H. (1985), 'The health effects of the transfer of technology to the developing world: report and case studies', in J. H. Ives (ed.), *The Export of Hazard* (London: Routledge & Kegan Paul), pp. 172–91.

Jackman, B. (1989), 'Kenya's bloody ivory', *Sunday Times Magazine*, 26 February, pp. 56–60.

Jenkins, R. (1987), *Transnational Corporations and Uneven Development* (London: Methuen).

Kidron, M., and Segal, R. (1984), *The New State of the World Atlas* (London: Pan).

Kitsuse, J. I., and Spector, M. (1981), 'The labeling of social problems', in E. Rubington and M. S. Weinberg (eds), *The Study of Social Problems* (New York: Oxford University Press), pp. 198–206.

Lappé, F. M., and Collins, J. (1982), *Food First* (London: Abacus).

Leonard, H. J. (1988), *Pollution and the Struggle for the World Product: Multinational Corporations, Environment, and International Comparative Advantage* (Cambridge: Cambridge University Press).

Levenstein, C., and Eller, S. W. (1985), 'Exporting hazardous industries: "for example" is not proof', in J. H. Ives (ed.), *The Export of Hazard* (London: Routledge & Kegan Paul), pp. 51–9.

Lever, H., and Huhne, C. (1985), *Debt and Danger: The World Financial Crisis* (Harmondsworth: Penguin).

Lindblom, C. E. (1980), *The Policy–Making Process*, 2nd edn (Englewood Cliffs, NJ: Prentice–Hall).

London Food Commission (1988), *Food Adulteration and How to Beat It* (London: Unwin Hyman).

London Food Commission (1989), *This Food Business* (London: Channel 4 and *New Statesman and Society*).

Lowe, P. (1983), 'Values and institutions in the history of British nature conservation', in A. Warren and F. B. Goldsmith (eds), *Conservation in Perspective* (Chichester: Wiley), pp. 329–52.

Lowe, P. (1988), 'Comparative "green" politics: the worldwide development of ecology parties', lecture given at Queen's University, Belfast, December.

Lowe, P. (1989), 'Gathering greens', *Marxism Today*, September, pp. 14–17.

Lowe, P., and Flynn, A. (1989), 'Environmental politics and policy in the 1980s', in J. Moran (ed.), *The Political Geography of Contemporary Britain* (London: Macmillan), pp. 255–79.

Lowe, P., and Goyder, J. (1983), *Environmental Groups in Politics* (London: Allen & Unwin).

Lowe, P., and Rüdig, W. (1986), 'Review article: political ecology and the social sciences – the state of the art', *British Journal of Political Science*, vol. 16, pp. 513–50.

McTaggart, D. (1978), *Greenpeace III. Journey into the Bomb* (London: Collins).

Michalowski, R. J., and Kramer, R. C. (1987), 'The space between laws: the problem of corporate crime in a transnational context', *Social Problems*, vol. 34, pp. 34–53.

Milbrath, L. W. (1984), *Environmentalists: Vanguard for a New Society* (Albany, NY: State University of New York Press).

Millstone, E. (1986), *Food Additives: Taking the Lid off what we Really Eat* (Harmondsworth: Penguin).

Moore, N. W. (1987), *The Bird of Time: The Science and Politics of Nature Conservation* (Cambridge: Cambridge University Press).

Müller–Rommel, F. (ed.) (1989), *New Politics in Western Europe: the Rise and Success of Green Parties and Alternative Lists* (Boulder, Colo: Westview).

National Audit Office (1990), *Bilateral Aid to India* (London: HMSO).

New Consumer (1989), 'Driving away the competition: concentration in the UK car market', *New Consumer*, vol. 1, pp. 26–7.

Newby, H. (1980), *Green and Pleasant Land* (Harmondsworth: Penguin).

Newby, H. (1988), *The Countryside in Question* (London: Hutchinson).

Nicholson, M. (1972), *The Environmental Revolution: A Guide for the New Masters of the World* (Harmondsworth: Penguin).

Nicholson, M. (1987), *The New Environmental Age* (Cambridge: Cambridge Unviersity Press).

North, R. (1986), *The Real Cost* (London: Chatto & Windus).

North, R. (1987), 'Greenpeace: still credible?', *The Independent*, 21 September 1987, p. 15.

Oteri, J. S., Weinberg, M. G., and Pinales, M. S. (1982), 'Cross–examination of chemists in drug cases', in B. Barnes and D. Edge (eds), *Science in Context* (Milton Keynes: Open University Press), pp. 250–9.

Paastale, J. (1989), 'Finland: the "Vihreät"', in Müller–Rommel (ed.), pp. 81–6.

Palmer, R., and Mahmood, M. (1988), 'Waste firms in toxic dumping racket', *The Sunday Times*, 20 November, p. 3.

Parker, D. (1989), 'Fly shippers', *Green Magazine*, vol. 1 (November), pp. 20–3.

Parkin, S. (1989), *Green Parties: An International Guide* (London: Heretic Books).

Paterson, T. (1989), *The Green Conservative: A Manifesto for the Environment* (London: Bow Publications).

Patterson, W. C. (1976), *Nuclear Power* (Harmondsworth: Penguin).

Pearce, D., Markandya, A., and Barbier, E. B. (1989), *Blueprint for a Green Economy* (London: Earthscan).

Pearce, F. (1989), *Turning up the Heat* (London: Paladin).

Pearce, F. (1990), 'Japan's licence to spend the earth', *Guardian*, 23 March, p. 27.

Pezzey, J. (1989), 'Greens and growth – a reply', *UK CEED Bulletin*, vol. 22, pp. 22–3.

Poguntke, T. (1989), 'The "new politics dimension" in European green parties', in F. Müller–Rommel (ed.), pp. 175–94.

Porritt, J. (1984), *Seeing Green: The Politics of Ecology Explained* (Oxford: Blackwell).

Porritt, J. (1988), 'Greens and growth', *UK CEED Bulletin*, vol. 19, pp. 22–3.

Porritt, J. (1989), 'Green shoots, rotten roots', *BBC Wildlife*, vol. 7, no. 6, pp. 352–3.

Porritt, J., and Winner, D. (1988), *The Coming of the Greens* (London: Fontana).

Prescott Allen, R. and C. (1988), *Genes from the Wild* (London: Earthscan).

Pugh, D. (1989), 'Getting into deep water', *Guardian*, 10 November, p. 29.

Pye–Smith, C., and Rose, C. (1984), *Crisis and Conservation: Conflict in the British Countryside* (Harmondsworth: Penguin).

Redclift, M. (1984), *Development and the Environmental Crisis: Red or Green Alternatives?* (London: Methuen).

Redclift, M. (1989), *Sustainable Development: Exploring the Contradictions* (London: Routledge).

Rootes, C. (1990), 'The future of the "New Politics": a European perspective', *Social Alternatives*, vol. 8, pp. 7–12.

Royal Society for Nature Conservation (1989a), *Creating a Better Future for Wildlife: Annual Review 1988–89* (Nettleham, Lincolnshire: RSNC).

Royal Society for Nature Conservation (1989b), *Losing Ground. Habitat Destruction in the UK: a Review in 1989* (Nettleham, Lincolnshire: RSNC).

Rüdig, W. (1986), 'Nuclear power: an international comparison of public protest in the USA, Great Britain, France and West Germany', in R. Williams and S. Mills (eds), *Public Acceptance of New Technologies: An International Review* (London: Croom Helm), pp. 364–417.

Samstag, T. (1988), *For Love of Birds* (Sandy, Bedfordshire: RSPB).

Schoon, N. (1990), 'Acid rain that earns Britain a black mark', *The Independent*, 26 March, p. 17.

Schoon, N., and Wilkie, T. (1988), 'The Greenhouse effect', *The Independent*, 17 October, p. 17.

Schwarz, W. (1989a), 'Victims of rape in paradise', *Guardian*, 13 March, p. 19.

Schwarz, W. (1989b), 'Now the good shall inherit', *Guardian*, 10 November, p. 27.

Searle, G. (1987), *Major World Bank Projects* (Camelford, Cornwall: Wadebridge Ecological Centre).

Secrett, C. (1988), 'Deadly offer poor countries find hard to refuse', *Guardian*, 15 July, p. 11.

Seddon, Q. (1989), *The Silent Revolution: Farming and the Countryside into the 21st Century* (London: BBC Books).

Seymour, J., and Girardet, H. (1987), *Blueprint for a Green Planet* (London: Dorling Kindersley).

Sheail, J. (1976), *Nature in Trust: the History of Nature Conservation in Britain* (Glasgow: Blackie).

Sheail, J. (1987), *Seventy–Five Years in Ecology: The British Ecological Society* (London: Blackwell).

Smith, R., and Wynne, B. (eds) (1988), *Expert Evidence: Interpreting Science in the Law* (London: Routledge).

Spector, M., and Kitsuse, J. I. (1977), *Constructing Social Problems* (Menlo Park, Calif.: Cummings).

Stevenson, J. (1984), *British Society 1914–45* (Harmondsworth: Penguin).

Stewart, F. (1978), *Technology and Underdevelopment*, 2nd edn (London: Macmillan).

Stott, M. (1984), 'Industrial pollution', *Links*, vol. 19, pp. 28–30.

Urwin, D. (1990), 'Green politics in Western Europe', *Social Studies Review*, vol. 5, no. 4, pp. 152–7.

Vaus, J. (1989), 'How green is the British public?', *UK CEED Bulletin*, vol. 26, pp. 10–11.

Vidal, J. (1990), 'Towards industrial evolution', *Guardian*, 12 January, p. 25.

Wainwright, M. (1989), 'Bugs in the system', *Guardian*, 15 December, p. 27.

Walker, P. (1989), 'Recycling', *Friends of the Earth Local Groups Newsletter*, vol. 178 (November), pp. 13–14.

Wallis, R. (1985), 'Science and pseudo–science', *Social Science Information*, vol. 24, pp. 585–601.

Walters, A. H. (1986), 'Nitrates in food', in E. Goldsmith and N. Hildyard (eds), *Green Britain or Industrial Wasteland?* (Cambridge: Polity), pp. 172–8.

Warnock, J. W. (1987), *The Politics of Hunger: The Global Food System* (London: Methuen).

Weber, M. (1964), *The Theory of Social and Economic Organization* (New York: Free Press).

Weir, D., and Shapiro, M. (1981), *Circle of Poison: Pesticides and People in a Hungry World* (San Francisco: Institute for Food and Development Policy).

Williams, N. (1989), 'Mad, bad and dangerous?', *Guardian*, 10 November, p. 10.

Williams, N. (1990a), 'Warming to ocean research', *Guardian*, 19 January, p. 27.

Williams, N. (1990b), 'A great stretch of the genes', *Guardian*, 4 May, p. 27.

Williamson, J. (1978), *Decoding Advertising: Ideology and Meaning in Advertising* (London: Marion Boyars).

World Commission on Environment and Development, (1987), *Our Common Future*, The Brundtland Report (Oxford: Oxford University Press).

Wynne, B. (1982), *Rationality and Ritual. The Windscale Inquiry and Nuclear Decisions in Britain* (Chalfont St Giles, Bucks.: British Society for the History of Science).

Yearley, S. (1988), *Science, Technology and Social Change* (London: Unwin Hyman).

Yearley, S. (1989), 'Bog standards: science and conservation at a public inquiry', *Social Studies of Science*, vol. 19, pp. 421–38.

Yoxen, E. (1983), *The Gene Business: Who Should Control Biotechnology?* (London: Pan).

Index

CITY OF DREAMS

...TURES IN THE

...RWORLD

Roman Myths

CITY OF DREAMS

For Clarisse

ORCHARD BOOKS
96 Leonard Street, London EC2A 4XD
Orchard Books Australia
14 Mars Road, Lane Cove, NSW 2066
This text was first published in Great Britain in the form of
a gift collection called *The Orchard Book of Roman Myths*,
illustrated by Emma Chichester Clark in 1999.
This edition first published in hardback in Great Britain in 2000
First paperback publication 2001
Text © Geraldine McCaughrean 1999
Illustrations © Tony Ross 2000
The rights of Geraldine McCaughrean to be identified as the author and
Tony Ross as the illustrator of this work have been asserted by them in
accordance with the Copyright, Designs, and Patents Act, 1988.
ISBN 1 84121 883 9 (hardback)
ISBN 1 84121 520 1 (paperback)
1 3 5 7 9 10 8 6 4 2 (hardback)
1 3 5 7 9 10 8 6 4 2 (paperback)
A CIP catalogue record for this book is available
from the British Library.
Printed in Great Britain